OFFICIAL AND UNOFFICIAL COURTS

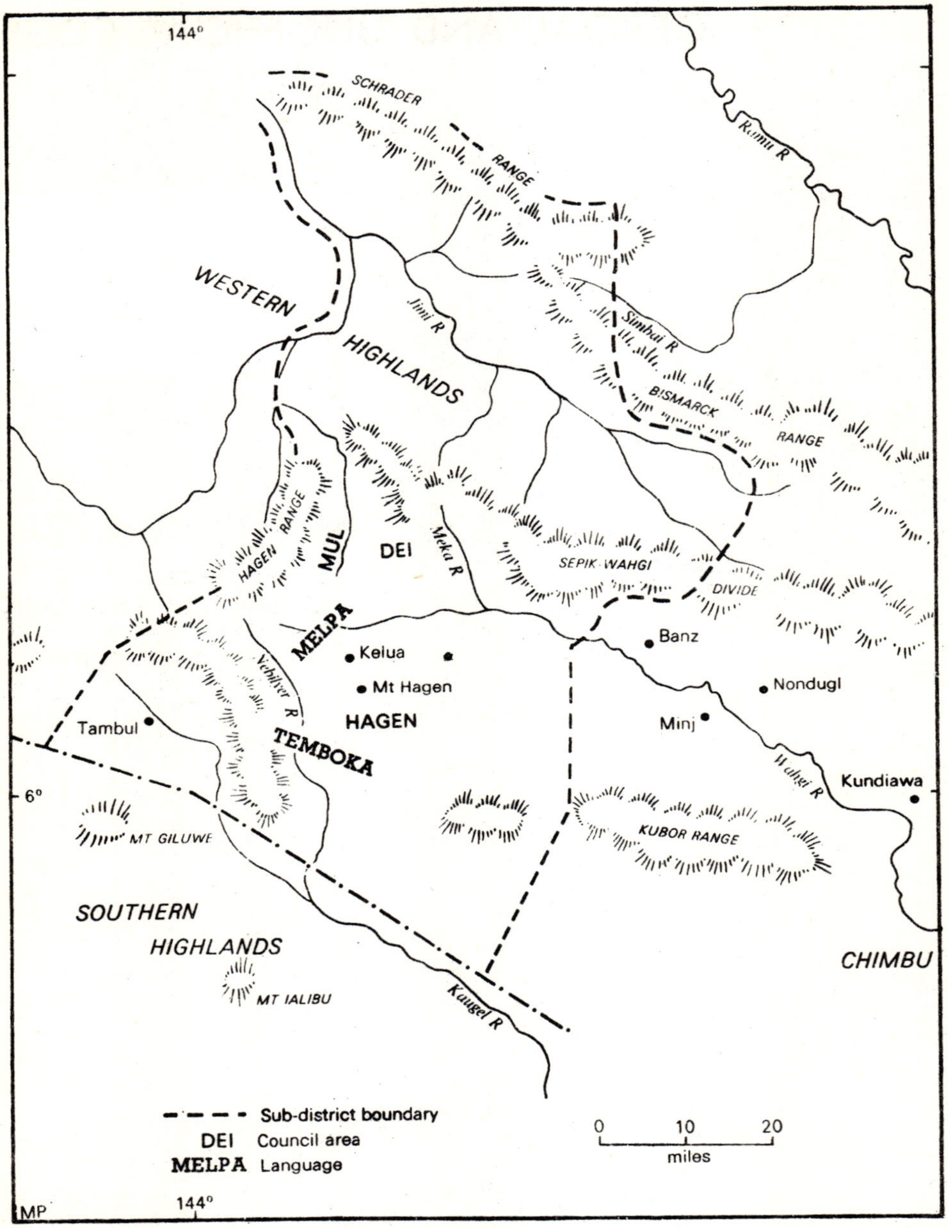

Fig. 1. Hagen sub-district

New Guinea Research Bulletin no. 47

OFFICIAL AND UNOFFICIAL COURTS

Legal assumptions and expectations in a highlands community

MARILYN STRATHERN

New Guinea Research Unit
The Australian National University
Port Moresby and Canberra

Printed and manufactured in Australia by Allens Printers, Canberra.

Cover design, Marlous Ploeg

National Library of Australia
card no. and ISBN 85818 011 1

Library of Congress Catalog
card no. 72-92324

Contents

Figures

Preface

> In the past we fought; now white men have come we sit down on the back of law. (An ageing Hagen big-man)

> Disputes are a universal feature of human social life. The central question [with what processes are we concerned in the field of law] thus becomes not do [a particular people] have law, but... in what ranges of social relationships do quarrels arise, what forms do they take, and by what means are they handled? (Epstein 1967:206)

The present Local Court in Papua New Guinea, writes B.J. Brown (1971:251), 'is not popular because it is not a people's court'. The people of Mount Hagen, in the Western Highlands District, are among those who still turn for the settlement of many disputes to quasi-traditional processes, including in some cases highly developed systems of unofficial 'courts'.

The existence of such 'villagers' courts' elsewhere has been interpreted as reflecting antipathy towards the official courts' structure:

> It is a disquietening fact that the indigenous community of TPNG has for many years been operating a widespread, completely unsupervised, and technically illicit legal system which has no contact with the Territory legal system. (Fenbury 1966:63)

A similar situation seems to have existed in relation to the Court of Native Affairs (hereafter CNA), the antecedent of the Local Court (Lawrence 1969:36). Epstein (1971:160-1) records how few Tolai in the 1960s took disputes to the CNA, but had developed vigorous dispute-settling forums of their own. Opposition to the official system is also described for the Nasioi of Bougainville, in their failure to utilise introduced legal processes (Momis and Ogan 1971:39; Ogan 1972:181); and Young (1971:140) observes that Goodenough Islanders had considerable doubts about the value of appeals to patrol officers. There may have been changes in these areas since they were studied, but they would not affect the comparison I wish to make with attitudes prevalent in Hagen.[1]

[1] In the following account I use 'Hagen' to refer generally to the sub-district and its inhabitants, 'Mt Hagen' for the town.

Very real differences exist between the operation of the official courts within the sub-district and the unofficial, technically illicit courts presided over by Hagen councillors and their adjutants. One might have expected that Hageners would turn to the latter as a viable institution 'of their own', while rejecting the former as an alien and imposed set of mechanisms of little pertinence to everyday affairs. Yet the common Hagen attitude is quite to the contrary: they treat the unofficial courts as part of the official system. This accords with their very extensive use of Administration agencies: DDA officers,[1] policemen, Local Court Magistrates - and in the past, CNA officials - have at times felt themselves inundated by the large number of issues brought to them for deliberation. While the Administration encourages the reporting of 'criminal' offences, it is significant that these are probably matched in number by 'civil' disputes, which are often handled with official reluctance. Hageners' willingness to take disputes to governmental bodies is connected with the manner in which they relate themselves to the new authority system. Their operation of unofficial courts is central to this.

Problems of law and order in Papua New Guinea have become the subject of recent public debate,[2] and the Department of Law is at present (1972) considering radical experimentation at the level of the Local Court.[3] The background to this is the whole problem of the adaptation of an essentially British legal system to Papua New Guinean conditions.[4] This study tries to present the viewpoint of a highlands community whose members are in their own way concerned with the 'problem' of law and order. My focus is on processes and procedures rather than the body of law as such. Fenbury (1966:65) points to the former as an area likely to contain problems of its own, in his quotation of a document presented to the British Parliament in 1960:

> But the British in Africa and elsewhere have sought not only to instil in the minds of the people their general principles of justice, which are wholly laudable, but also to impose their main processes

---

[1] Officers of the Division of District Administration within the Department of the Administrator.

[2] See, for example, Watts (1972).

[3] For example, see statment by the Secretary for Law to the House of Assembly, 8 June 1971 (House of Assembly Debates, vol.II, no.14, pp.4325-6).

[4] For some recent commentaries, see Rowley (1965:ch.4), Barnett (1967) and (in press), B.J. Brown (1969), and Oram (1970).

> of law in circumstances which are entirely different to those in which they were evolved.... Has there not been a mistaken tendency to count judicial procedure with the administration of justice?

Hageners' present-day concern with processes of dispute-settlement is one aspect of their general reaction to various imposed institutions. The extent to which the introduced legal system is regarded as relevant to the settlement of the kinds of contentious issues that arise in a Hagen community is partly related to the degree of legitimacy with which Hageners invest the Administration as a whole.

The Hagen area was chosen for study on the basis of familiarity. I had spent sixteen months there in 1964-65 and another two in 1967. Fieldwork for this study was carried out between September 1970 and January 1971.[1] Had it been planned later, it might have taken a rather different shape, and dealt in detail with the widely publicised confrontations and incidents of violence which occurred, in 1971 and 1972, between Hageners and Europeans, and between tribal groups.[2] But the present investigation would still have had to be done. In it I concentrate on Hageners' attitudes to the legal system as these emerge from their handling of everyday disputes. Some of these are 'minor', but others are ones which in the past might have escalated to the point at which groups felt impelled to go to war. I am concerned to some extent, then, with processes that prevent the escalation of disputes.

Several events dramatised Hagen as a 'problem area' for law and order in 1971 and early 1972. These included reports of fighting over land, reprisals ('payback') following alleged responsibility for deaths, violence in the town of Mt Hagen, and the negotiation of a large compensation settlement with a European ('extortion').[3] Europeans in Hagen were already concerned over a reportedly mounting crime rate, especially of crimes with violence, and especially in the town itself.[4] Other disturbing trends were

---

[1] There have been changes in Hagen since 1970 - as, for example, in the number of full-time Local Court Magistrates working in the town - but except where these are specifically mentioned, the ethnographic present is 1970.

[2] Some of these are described in A.J. Strathern (1972b).

[3] See, for example, the Post-Courier for 9 February 1971, 27 July 1971, 29 November 1971, 14 December 1971, 17 December 1971, 8 February 1972 and 9 February 1972.

[4] Post-Courier, 11 August 1971.

displays of aggression towards Europeans and the police, and an apparently increasing tendency for Hageners to take the law into their own hands and settle issues by fighting. To the Hageners there seemed to be spiralling provocations to violent action - including widespread drinking, and deaths from road accidents - unprecedented since pacification.[1] But there also appears to have been a general withdrawal in rural areas from the practice of seeking out officials to adjudicate in matters of dispute. All these events suggest that the Administration's legitimacy is losing ground. Europeans interpret them as evidence of breakdown in law and order.

The phrase 'law and order' obscures some important issues. It would probably be true to say that throughout the 1960s Hageners had not only accepted the Administration's centralisation of force but more or less concurred in it as a condition of what was introduced to them as progress. The fact that groups who in the past would frequently have engaged in warfare no longer did so was accompanied by an acknowledgment that for a number of offences the state ('the law', 'the *kiap*', 'the district office') would mete out punishment. The official judicial system was in many, though not all, circumstances seen as a valid alternative to Hageners' own settlement procedures. When quasi-traditional methods were used, overt verbal reference was often made to the workings of the official courts and the 'law' they promulgated. To a large extent this still holds true for minor disputes. One can argue that Hageners have assimilated the notion of 'law'. As a concept, it is widely understood.

'Order' is another matter. After forty years of colonisation, the traditional political structure of Hagen tribes and clans is still an important dimension in public affairs. In the names of the clans and tribes to which they belong, individuals compete with one another, come into conflict, feel threatened, Almost any dispute in the past could escalate to political proportions, and all major troubles between large-scale groups today carry implications of political aggression. Traditional procedures for dealing with such troubles embraced both 'dispute-settlement' and 'political action'. This latter area lies outside the competence of the official courts.[2] Troubles arise nowadays at the

---

[1] Such provocations are well recognised by DDA officials in Hagen (*Post-Courier*, 9 February 1972).

[2] Members of DDA have official competence in this sphere. In working to secure effective solutions to Hageners' political problems, they may utilise traditional techniques (see e.g., *Post-Courier*, 18 February 1972).

level of intergroup relations where traditional peace-keeping controls never operated before or rarely operated successfully.[1] Traditional controls are also inadequate in coping with the modern scale of confrontations created by council boundaries and the like. The concept of law may be appealed to during intercouncil conflicts, but carries little force where it is unrelated to effective settlement procedures. It seems that the idea of 'law' has most firmly taken root in those fairly stable contexts where traditional controls did (and do) operate with some success. In the realm of small-scale disputes it is a powerful idiom which invests what are still partly traditional processes with an outlook of modernism.

If Hageners have turned away from official judicial procedures in handling major crises, it is because these do not recognise the problems for 'order' which major crimes in Hagen often precipitate - how to maintain orderly relations between groups thrown into imbalance. It is essential to recall here the segmentary nature of Hagen society, in which clans and tribes see themselves as pitting power and prestige against one another. Where inequalities are created, resort is increasingly being made to force as a means of redress.

Use of force should not be confused with lawlessness. In Hagen hands, such use naturally threatens Administration control of it. But what in official terms appears to be a breakdown of 'order', from the Hagen point of view may be an attempt to cope with a situation where order is already threatened (e.g., by a fatal car accident where one group [the victim's] has suffered at the hands of another [the driver's or owner's]). The situation has analogies with the colonial persecution of witch-finders in parts of Africa. It is the style of indigenous settlement procedures that often seems repugnant to Europeans, to whom revenge epitomises the primitive, and financial transactions seem mercenary if not corrupt. But behind these procedures may lie precisely the imperatives to abide by rules, resolve conflicts, punish offenders and exact justice that lie behind the rule of law.[2] Moreover, dispute-settlement procedures are socially 'necessary'[3] in a way that economic development or a national constitution are not. Commonsense tells people that officials cannot delve into every issue which arises, and cannot solve problems they do not

---

[1] A point emphasised to me by Andrew Strathern: a number of the ideas presented here I owe to our joint discussions.

[2] Cf. B.J. Brown (1969:183).

[3] See Oram (1970:11).

appreciate. It is meaningless to condemn their own procedures as wrong or bad or primitive, and it would have to be demonstrated that the principles on which they rest are utterly alien to the concept of justice.

My main concern is with types of disputes to which Administration agencies and the ideas promulgated by the judiciary are still seen as largely relevant. Yet what on a political scale precipitates crises also permeates settlement procedures at the lowest level. I refer here to the mutually conflicting notions held by Hageners and by Administration officials of their respective judicial capacities. In paying attention to relatively minor disputes, the ones that do not escalate, I am dealing with an area in which many Hageners actually think of themselves as adjusting to Administration requirements, and in which the gap between their perception of the judicial system and the official point of view is for that reason perhaps the more striking.

Limitations of the inquiry

This study is concerned primarily with the actions and ideas of Hageners and focuses in particular on their unofficial courts. Cases presented are mainly those dealt with by such bodies, whose workings are probably less widely known than those of the official courts. As has been indicated, little is said about issues relating to recent homicides, or to land disputes, a relatively new phenomenon. Another important area outside its scope is urban crime: Mt Hagen, with its growing migrant population and the particular facilities it offers, would be a study in itself. My remarks concern those whose livelihood is still essentially a rural one.

In describing reactions, I am necessarily judging from acquaintance with a small number of individuals. As I suggest later, men prominent in dispute-settlement follow idiosyncratic styles; there are also differences between local regions, especially in respect of distance from Mt Hagen. I have drawn on my general knowledge of the Mt Hagen and Dei Council areas,[1] but most of the conclusions will also apply to Mul Council and the part of the Nebilyer Valley which has only recently joined Mt Hagen Council. However, specific fieldwork was done in the vicinity of Kelua (Kelua no.1), about eight miles by road from Mt Hagen; the attitudes I describe in most detail are those of men of the Elti, Penambe, Ndika and Yamka tribes. They have had experience of Europeans from the early days of exploration and are within

---

[1] There are several local government councils within the Hagen sub-district, one council appropriating the name 'Mt Hagen'.

easy access of the facilities of the town, including the central police station and court-house. In more outlying parts, as, for example, the M^{e}ka Valley[1] in the Dei Council area which is served by a council-house complex, with visiting magistrate, council adviser and rural police station, knowledge of the agencies situated in town is poorer, and the judicial facilities are probably used less readily. Here also there is a more dogmatic emphasis on settling disputes locally.

At points the account is oversimplified. The chapter on traditional modes of dispute-settlement, for example, is no more than a discussion of principles relevant to an understanding of the unofficial courts, and I give little supporting evidence for my statements. Pseudonyms are given in all case-histories but in only one instance (as indicated) are facts also disguised.

In the official system my concern is with the Local rather than District or Supreme Courts. I have found it simplest to follow Hageners' usage of the terms 'court', which they apply both to official Administration courts and unofficial hearings conducted by local councillors or <u>komiti</u>. This is not, of course, Administration usage. When I refer to Local Court, however, I mean the official body. (Hageners sometimes refer to their unofficial courts as 'local court' but I do not use it in this way.) The Department of Law's Local Court Magistrate in Hagen is referred to as the LCM, while officials of the Division of District Administration (who may also hold appointments as Local Court Magistrates) are referred to by the colloquial term <u>kiap</u>.

Finally, I take as a base for analysis all formal institutions involved in 'dispute-settling' rather than the judicial system as such. The Local Court is among these institutions, but they also include other Administration, as well as indigenous, agencies.

<u>Acknowledgments</u>

Most of the fieldwork on which this Bulletin is based was carried out while I was a Research Fellow with the New Guinea Research Unit of The Australian National University.

There are many people in Papua New Guinea whom I must thank for their assistance. I would not have progressed very far without the unstinting services of Oke, and the talks I had

---

[1] The following symbols are used in this Bulletin: raised ^{e} - a mid, close, central, unrounded vowel (the schwa), as the first vowel in English 'banana'; and ϕ - a mid, open, front, rounded vowel, as in German 'hören'.

with *Luluai* Tetep and *Luluai* Aepto, Wundake, Councillor Noke and Councillor Ongka, *Komiti* Køya, *Komiti* Yakomb, *Komiti* Ropra and *Komiti* Kerwa, and with Ru and Nykint. Magistrate Andrew Maino gave generously of his time and I must thank him and Brian O'Neill, Resident Magistrate, for their very real help whenever I visited the court-house in Mt Hagen. I also appreciate help I received in Mt Hagen from Len Aisbett, acting District Commissioner, Roger Gleeson, then acting Assistant District Commissioner, and Dick Olive, then Adviser to Dei Council; from A.T. Allison, Welfare Officer; from John Rorosi Matalale, then Administrative Officer for Mt Hagen Council, and Simon Apa, Clerk for Dei Council; and from Superintendent Dutton and Inspector Briancourt of the police force.

I have benefited considerably from the encouragement and comments of the Honourable Mr Justice J.P. Minogue, and from discussions with Tos Barnett, then of the Department of Law, University of Papua and New Guinea, who has also read drafts of the Bulletin in various forms. I am grateful, too, for detailed comments on parts of the draft from Andrew Maino, Roger Gleeson, Professor Ann Chowning and Professor Bill Epstein.

Finally, I must record my gratitude to various bodies for allowing me to use and in some instances quote from their records: the Department of the Administrator, the Department of Law, the Department of Social Development and Home Affairs, and Mt Hagen Local Government Council.

Chapter 1

Traditional dispute-settlement

> You don't listen to what is said - you steal, you are always getting into trouble, so what is in your mind, then? (An elderly Hagener's recollection of what would be said to an inveterate thief)

> We use rhetorical language for public speeches, but we shouldn't be using it for the words a court has to say! (Interpolation from the audience at an unofficial court hearing)

Hageners' expectations about the functions of official courts are derived partly from the manner in which many of their own processes of settlement work. In addition, their understanding of the Local, District and Supreme Courts, and demands made on them by the Administration, have caused them to modify what traditional procedures they still follow, and have led to the emergence of a regular dispute-settling agency, in the form of councillors' courts, that is very much a mixture of the new and the old.

Hageners are aware that the Administration regards itself as pre-empting the right to deal with certain offences, notably homicide.[1] Other issues are seen to be completely outside the scope of the official courts. Among these are treatment of the social causes of sickness (sickness, it is believed, may be sent by ancestral ghosts to bring certain wrongs to light); allegations concerning the administration of poison; and punishment of offences connected with menstrual pollution (females are responsible for the fact that careless behaviour during menstruation brings danger to the male community). Councillors' courts may deal with such matters, but actually tend to spend most time on issues in which official courts also take an interest: for example, theft, quarrelling

---

[1] Strictly the official courts tend to take notice of only some aspects of homicide (punishment of the culprit, etc.) while leaving other aspects (e.g., group liability) to out-of-court settlement.

which verges on assault, damage to property by livestock, bridewealth and other debts, and suits for divorce. The way in which Hageners themselves attempt to handle these disputes shows both the extent to which they have absorbed introduced notions about 'law' and understand the functioning of the introduced courts, and the extent to which they still rely on indigenous methods of settlement.

Hagen society

The majority of people who live in the Hagen sub-district speak one of two closely related languages: Melpa (or 'Hagen') and the Temboka dialect of Gawigl (Wurm 1964). Together Melpa and Temboka encompass a population of perhaps 75,000 Hageners. Early studies of Hageners were made by Vicedom (Vicedom and Tischner 1943-48) and Ross (e.g., Ross 1936), both missionaries, and later by Strauss (Strauss and Tischner 1962). Vicedom and Strauss give accounts of traditional means of dispute-settlement. Some material is also presented in A.M. Strathern (1972).[1]

Europeans first established a camp some miles from the present Mt Hagen township, at what is now known as Kelua no.2, in 1933-34. At that time warfare had caused a number of population movements in the area. Near the camp itself a tract of land had been abandoned by one group, and was being taken over by refugees from another. A strong coalition of their enemies had forced them to flee, and many of the refugees were in a precarious situation. Looking back on those days, one or two men now describe how afraid

---

[1] Vicedom and Ross provide general ethnographic accounts, particularly interesting because of their experience of the area from the 1930s. Strauss adds a dimension in his refinement of religious concepts. A.M. Strathern (1972) deals with women's roles and includes a discussion of traditional and modern dispute-settlement as a context in which to analyse women's rights and status. Of relevance to the present chapter is its description of types of compensation payments, and some account of the structure of judicial liability, which I do not further discuss here. A.J. Strathern (1971) is concerned primarily with ceremonial exchange and the phenomenon of big-men, and with warfare and political relations between clans and tribes, while A.J. Strathern (1972a) analyses group structure in terms of ideology and recruitment processes. Mention should also be made of works which specifically treat aspects of social change, e.g. Sinha (1969) on cash cropping, A.J. Strathern (1970) on the roles of councillors; recent or current work includes as yet unpublished studies by Rowe (local government councils) and Shand (nucleus estates).

they were to go and observe the new arrivals - not only because the Europeans were feared to be cannibal spirits but because to venture from their settlements might place the men at the mercy of their enemies. Since peace was imposed by the Administration, this particular group have recovered from the threat of extinction, reassembled many of their members under the representation of a single councillor, and have not only consolidated their claims to the land they now occupy but have expanded into formerly underpopulated territories. They both recognise the Administration's advent as instrumental in their survival and are proud of their present strength.[1]

A number of points here indicate salient features of Hagen Society. Named groups are crucial for reference: the most encompassing category is the tribe. Throughout the Hagen area there are perhaps seventy tribes, ranging in population from under 500 to over 5,000. They occupy territories, though these are not necessarily continuous areas of land. Within the tribe is a hierarchy of further named groups; precise internal arrangements differ, but the clan tends to be a primary point of identification. Except in the very smallest of tribes, the clan is exogamous, often occupies a single stretch of territory, and is the most important group for the organisation of corporate activities such as fighting (in the past), conducting public exchanges of valuables, and (in the 1960s) buying cars. In the initial establishment of councils in the Hagen area (Mt Hagen Council 1961, Kui 1962, Dei 1963),[2] the clan formed the basis of council constituencies.

Clans (numbering on average 200 to 300 persons) are themselves composed of varying combinations of subgroups. The smallest of these ('lineage') is differentiated from the others by the derivation of its name, taken directly from its founding ancestor. These eponymous ancestors are genealogically thought to have lived one or two generations before present senior men. Although assertions may be made that the whole clan, or even the whole tribe, is also descended from 'one father', the links are not genealogically demonstrable. In fact, at all levels this kind

---

[1] In 1970 they and an associated group gave a dancing display: it was too grand for their own ceremonial ground and they commandeered the former Mt Hagen airstrip.

[2] Mt Hagen and Kui were merged in December 1964 to form a joint Mt Hagen Council, while in the same year Mul Council was also established. With the further expansion of Mt Hagen Council to include Temboka-speakers from the Nebilyer Valley in 1968, the three councils now serve most of the Melpa and Temboka regions.

of statement should be taken largely as a matter of ideology, which emphasises but one aspect of group recruitment. Men also are to be found living with their mother's clansmen or in other groups. Most individuals are concerned to maintain a large network of ties with kinsmen outside their clan. Many of these links are created through marriage and are sustained by exchanges of gifts or contributions to enterprises. At marriage a woman usually resides with the husband in the group of his residence and for some purposes may be considered a 'member' of his clan, for others a 'member' of her natal clan.

Clans may be regularly linked with other clans, both within their tribe and outside it. Intensive intermarriage is often a basis for such a link, which may develop into a politically significant alliance. Allied groups conduct ceremonial exchanges with one another, and in the past provided help in warfare. It is a feature of Hagen society that coalitions of alliances can embrace groups numbering thousands of people. But the divergent interests of individual clans, and other factors involved in ceremonial exchange and the structuring of enemy relations, meant that in the past there were always limits to hostile activity. Warfare was formerly endemic in the sense that it was a means of action to which people might at any time turn, but it was certainly not continuous, and major routs such as the one referred to earlier were not common.

A number of checks upon individuals prevented an immediate recourse to arms in the face of trouble. For example, within the clan, fighting was recognised but discouraged: if it broke out, attempts were made to restrict the weapons to 'non-lethal' items such as wooden sticks. This rule was sometimes invoked between close allies, or between clans from within a common tribe. Fighting outside the clan, however, did not receive consistent discouragement, so that any ally might turn into an enemy. Allies who on occasion were also enemies ('minor enemies') usually restricted their arms to weapons that were at hand - axes or spears - and would desist at the first death, or fail to renew fighting after a day or two. Very importantly, settlement could be achieved through an exchange of wealth. But enemies who were never allies ('major enemies') were always vulnerable to attack, for settlement was very unlikely and there were always grievances outstanding. Men away from their home territory would be ambushed, and attack from poison was a constant fear. Battle involved not only war regalia but the full complement of weapons - shields, spears, arrows fitted with warheads, and battle axes. It could be waged indefinitely, the only retaliation for death being the infliction of further injury.

The past tense is appropriate here since the Administration has banned warfare, although the clashes referred to in the preface and other recent (1970 on) displays of strength closely resemble traditional warfare activity. But the political relations of a generation ago are still very relevant for present-day ties between groups and generate, among other things, competitive displays such as the dance festival mentioned above.

Competition and rivalry mark relations between individual men as well as between groups. There were no traditional offices of leadership, and consequently no positions which gave persons authority over others outside close kin relations. Eminence in public affairs was shown primarily in a man's ability as a manager - not only in the management of resources which gave him the wealth with which to make prestigious displays, but in the management of people, so that he was seen to influence decisions or to take a lead that others would follow. Such 'big-men' depended on verbal skills, words being used to impress, to present a point of view, to cajole and persuade. Big-men were contrasted in their techniques with those who tried to achieve their ends by violence alone. A 'violent man' rushed headlong into a fray, whereas a 'big-man' would weigh up the situational advantages of using force as against other methods. This was not a society where fighting ability alone brought prestige. Dispute-settlement in the past gave the big-man scope to test and display his influence.

Fighting, ceremonial exchange and dispute-settlement, like other public affairs, were primarily the concern of men. Women's importance lay elsewhere. They were (and still are) responsible for much of the day-to-day work associated with growing the staple sweet potato, and played a major role in planting and harvesting most food crops. Men's contribution, chiefly in the form of labour in clearing gardens and building fences, was irregular, and is nowadays not particularly time-consuming. Women also tended pigs, the chief domestic animal and a very significant item of wealth. Ceremonial exchange (_moka_) was a prime context in which the pig was used. Many types of transactions came under the rubric _moka_, but the basic element was a delayed exchange of valuables involving notions of increment which brought each partner prestige. It might be conducted between individuals privately, or clan members associate together as a body to synchronise exchanges with members of other groups. Often group exchanges combined _moka_ with warfare compensation payments (either indemnity for losses to a minor enemy or reimbursement of allies). Shells were also wealth objects. Pigs and shells were used in a host of transactions such as bridewealth, funeral payments and compensations. Pigs were sacrificed to ancestral ghosts. Women's claim to a control over shells was much less than over pigs, but they had some status as persons whose marriages linked individual affines and in turn the respective clans. Although only a few men (about one-fifth) were able to marry more than one wife, polygyny was something of an ideal.

With the introduction of cash cropping in coffee and now tea, the growth of markets, the local availability of jobs in the expanding Mt Hagen township, as well as labour schemes which take young men away from the area, Australian currency has now superseded shells and Hageners envisage a future without them. Where there is a choice, they are interested on the whole in enterprises which increase their own 'businesses' rather than in wage-earning; for this reason there has been a decline since the early 1960s in labour seeking employment on local plantations. Some Hageners have hired their own labourers for enterprises such as clearing land for coffee, while it is a widespread ambition for men to own a truck or passenger vehicle.

Christian activity, mainly through Lutheran and Roman Catholic missions, has been a feature since the early days of contact, although there is still broad acknowledgment of ancestral ghosts, who look after the affairs of their descendants and maintain an interest in clan morality. Visiting persons with sickness is a chief means by which both the ghosts and God are thought to indicate their attitudes towards human behaviour.

Settlement procedures

Hageners had no traditional system of courts - specialist institutions that gave persons authority to adjudicate in matters of dispute - nor even regularly convened moots at which troubles were aired. Nevertheless, in their handling of trouble cases they did recognise three processes which in combination gave rise to a court-like situation: non-violent confrontation of disputants willing to talk out rather then fight out their grievances; interference of big-men as arbiters or mediators; and adjustment of claims through compensation payments. These were only some of the traditional methods (others included self-help backed by threat of force, armed retaliations, self-inflicted injury, and appeal to supernatural sanctions). Apparent similarities between Local Court processes and traditional settlement by negotiation, mediation and compensation have probably facilitated Hageners' own adaptation of official procedure in the councillors' unofficial courts; this, however, is largely unrecognised. Hageners do compare the official and unofficial courts, but in terms of modernity. Both are manifestations of the new 'law'. They tend to overstress the differences between 'the past' and 'now', and to underplay very real continuities. Such a view emerges from explicit statements, particularly from the manner in which they represent the impact of European culture on their own. Yet there were elements in traditional procedures which find echoes in the official courts system, and on which, whether recognising it[1] or not, people lean heavily in their unofficial courts.

Traditionally offences were seen as actions against individuals, or collectivities of individuals, rather than against 'society' or 'humanity' as a whole. Offences could be looked upon as being against specific clans or tribes but these were not the total 'society'. There were no crimes for which a person would be prosecuted per se that did not also take into account the necessity to remedy an injury inflicted upon another. There were, however, situations in which general outrage would be expressed, although specific individuals were still the most offended. Wayward and capricious behaviour on the part of women was often viewed by men as a threat to some of their crucial social arrangements (such as affinal alliances), and what was interpreted as female aggression - flagrant sexual promiscuity or use of poison - brought retaliation that had strong punitive elements. Punishment was also prominent in the reaction to serious delicts within the clan, such as homicide or theft, or assault between closely related blood kin. Here the supposed punitive agents included ancestral ghosts; punishment could be allayed by confession.

While the notion of punishment was not foreign to Hageners, there was no specific body which could administer it in a disinterested way. It was simply an element, of more or less prominence, in the satisfaction sought by offended individuals.[2] Most dispute-settlement procedures were self-help measures. As Lawrence (1969:30) has written in general of Papua New Guinea: 'The individual whose rights have been infringed must himself initiate and carry through retaliatory action with whatever support he can get from clansmen, kinsmen, affines, and other associates'.

---

[1] I do not wish to overemphasise the lack of recognition; it may be that the continuities are self-evident to Hageners or that they do not require explanation or dogmatic formulation as does the imposition of novel procedures. Aspects of unofficial court procedure may be referred to as 'our way of doing things', but one often hears denials that anything like a court existed in the past.

[2] Ancestors who punish intraclan delicts are regarded as angry and as themselves offended persons.

Self-help which took the form of single-handed retaliation, or concerted action by a set of people with identical interests, shaded into efforts to seek the support of persons with diverse interests. Here more justification might be required of the plaintiff,[1] and an appeal might be made to a wider range of public values. There is some contrast between the following two reactions to theft. Both were accounts given to me in 1965 of disputes said to have arisen at about the time white men arrived.

> A man killed a pig belonging to someone from a neighbouring and friendly clan of a different tribe. The owner of the pig, along with his clan brothers, followed the trail of blood till they discovered where the pig had been cooked and eaten. They were armed with sticks and, calling in men of a brother clan to help them, attacked the thieves. The fighting lasted for a day, ceasing inconclusively at nightfall. No further action was taken.[2]

> A theft again occurred between the same two clans. The owner of the pig was a big-man, who happened to reside on the tribal territory of the thief's group, for he had sent a sister in marriage there and obtained wives for himself from this group. The pig-owner and his clan brothers, armed with sticks, confronted the thief and his clansmen who at once agreed to settlement, urged on by big-men of their own clan and of another clan of their tribe. In order to re-establish friendly relations, the thief's clansmen offered to make <u>moka</u>[3] out of their compensation, handing over a massive gift of shells and live pigs; the owner's clan subsequently reciprocated with cooked pig.

These two thefts occurred in similar social contexts. The difference lies in the threshold of self-help. In the first case

---

[1] I use the terms defendant and plaintiff to refer to disputants in the position of accused and accuser (and their positions could be reversed within the course of debate).

[2] It is doing the case some injustice to extract it from its context, which was a bout of thefts between the clans following an initial grievance over failure to pay indemnity for a wound received while the one was aiding the other as allies in war.

[3] See p.13. By converting the compensation payments into a pretext for mutual ceremonial exchange, the desire for public reconciliation was made explicit.

it was not until after a day's battle that the pig-owner was encouraged by his tired clansmen to give up, because they were afraid of instigating a major conflict. He may have subsequently taken private revenge but without the support of his brothers. In the second case the owner's display of force did not go beyond a threat, largely because of his position and prominence and his personal relations with big-men on the other side, upon whose interests he was able to play. They would be anxious to placate the plaintiff but highly unlikely themselves to take physical retaliation on the thief, their own clansman. The result was a generous compensation payment. Owners in both these cases instigated retaliation, but in the second force was dropped quickly as a means of coercion and the case was settled by reference to the recognised claims of the big-man and the long-term advantages of peace between the two clans.

The nature of the reaction to an offence depended not so much upon its type (whether it was theft, arson or adultery), as on its relative scale and on the relationship between offender and victim. A minor theft between brothers might be glossed over, whereas a major one would be cause for outrage; between persons distantly related, satisfaction might have to be gained in either case. Again, spouses might suffer insults and casual quarrelling with indifference, itself an index of their intimacy, where kinsmen might receive offence. But if the quarrelling escalated to a pitch that threatened the continuity of the relationship, differences had to be resolved. Unresolved quarrelling between actual clansmen supposedly led to the interference of ghosts, who showed displeasure through sending sickness and demanded sacrifice as a demonstration of the restored relationship. The clan ghosts of husband and wife could send sickness to their joint children. Often people were content merely to analyse the situation in mechanistic terms: 'the quarrel itself brought on the illness'.

Where the aim was restoration of a relationship, it was inappropriate for the contenders to aggravate their troubles by hasty recourse to violence. Especially between close blood kin or members of a single clan, retaliation in the form of fighting, assault, abuse and so on, was regarded as simply exacerbating disputes,[1] because it threatened fundamental ties out of all proportion to the original offence.

---

[1] It is recognised that the initial offence may be the result of some provocation: A has a grudge against B and steals from his garden (rather than someone else's), and B is only adding to the original fault against A by physically attacking the latter after the theft. In the same way as A's retaliation by theft is seen as out of proportion to the cause of his grudge, so B's retaliation by assault is seen as out of proportion to the theft.

In disputes concerning persons of different clans who were not related through marriage or did not have close residential association, the notion of a proportionate or 'just' (kapokla) retaliation varied with political relations. Between friendly clans (allies and minor enemies) efforts to achieve at least a modus vivendi might lead to willingness on the victim's part to accept compensation without inflicting further punishment, and desire on the offender's part to make a generous settlement. Nevertheless, fighting between such groups was not under the same control as within a single clan, and aggressive incidents such as theft or adultery themselves modified the character of the prevailing political relationship. Major enemies, on the other hand, rarely resolved disputes to mutual satisfaction (kapokla), individual offences being overshadowed by the long-standing imbalance of past conflicts. Almost any trouble could become a pretext for armed attack, and once conflict had begun other issues such as unavenged homicide swung into focus.

Procedures for gaining satisfaction can be ranged along a continuum according to the scale of physical force involved. This is an illuminating scale to choose, since governmental centralisation of major use of physical force limits what traditional processes are still effective. Main points in the continuum may be summarised as follows: (i) The two parties might reveal the cause of their complaints about each other and patch up their quarrel on the grounds of this revelation. (ii) Agreement to patch up a quarrel might be marked by an exchange of goods or a unilateral payment to restore the balance between them, sometimes made willingly, but sometimes grudgingly or in response to the threat of desperate action. (iii) Demand for compensation could be refused, so that the plaintiff resorted to force to seize what he considered adequate recompense, or secretly plotted revenge in the form of a counter-offence (e.g., retaliatory theft or rape). (iv) Without going through the steps of requesting satisfaction, the offended person might at once turn to revenge, or would see the attack on himself (and/or his fellows) as justification for launching warfare. In the course of fighting the offender and his clansmen would suffer (Melpa 'feel') for their crime.

At any of these stages an individual might be helped by others, or persons act to seek joint satisfaction for a common injury. When people met to discuss settlement they were often accompanied by supporters, and the meeting would attract spectators. (Such assemblies were ad hoc arrangements: there was no regularly convened body before which disputes could be brought.) At any of these points, too, big-men might interfere, in some cases encouraging conflict, in others actively trying to impose restraint.

Modern accounts of past events attribute to big-men the characteristic of especially encouraging people to come to peaceful settlement through material compensation. There was thus a tendency for three elements to go together: verbal negotiation, intervention by prominent leaders, and resolution of the issue through payments. These were the elements I identified as leading to a court-like situation, and which survive as processes in modern Hagen. For this reason they deserve further attention.

Talk, big-men and payments

Talk. The place of verbal negotiation in the settlement of disputes is seen in the wide-ranging referents of the term ik ('talk, speech, language'). It was used for the homily with which big-men rounded off the settlement of a case (ik man ngonom, 'he gives talk'), reminding persons of their obligations and pointing out where their 'true' interests lay. The oratorical capacity of big-men to use words persuasively, their ability to argue the truth out of someone, made them ik nitimin wu^{e} mbø ('men who talk'); submission to or agreement with their decisions on the part of listeners was ik pili ('to hear talk'). In a wider sense, the phrase ik pili indicated the acceptance of norms, an inveterate social nuisance being one who 'did not listen'. Where people were persuaded of or admitted the validity of an argument, the 'talk caught them' (ik titim). 'Your talk can't catch me; it is like smoke', was said of someone who failed to prove his case. Ik referred not only to techniques of verbal persuasion but to the whole process of argument and dialogue itself, and before the introduction of the now Melpa-ised word kot (Pidgin for court), peaceful hearings were 'compensation-talk' (e.g., wu^{e} kumøp ik, 'talk over the man's restitution (kumøp)'). Ik embraced both the fact of dispute or argument and the cause of dispute or the necessity to have an argument. Thus ik petem ('talk lies there') or ik ninimin ('words are spoken') could mean 'there is trouble'. Should a person's grievance be smouldering away after an incident had apparently been closed, others said of him that 'he still has talk', 'his talk is not finished'.

The process of eliciting the cause of a dispute was ik para ndui ('to open up the talk')[1] or ik øki ('to dig out the talk').[2] A defendant might begin his speech with the declaration, 'Now I shall speak, and bring the talk outside' (ik-e aket tep namb).

---

[1] The same phrase later used for the 'opening up' of the Hagen area by the Administration.

[2] As sweet potatoes were dug from the soil; a similar metaphor referred to 'lifting out' the talk in the manner of cooked food being removed from an earth oven.

This phraseology rested on the notion that the root of the trouble lay beneath surface arrangements and was to be excavated and brought to light: ik pukl mana petem ('the root of the talk lies below'). Sometimes ik pukl was synonymous with ik peng ('the head of the talk'); at other times the root was contrasted with the head as basic issues were contrasted with a general narrative of event. Pukl (lit. 'root' or 'base', as of a tree or root crop) could be used of links between people or things, including causal relationships.[1] It was more than a statement of fact: it connected events in a manner which suggested their explanation. In the judicial context it could be glossed as 'truth'. Judicial truth in Hagen was the revelation of a person's motives and thus also of his state of mind (noman). The 'reason' (pukl) for an angry gesture lay in the person's reaction to whatever provoked it.[2]

In searching for the root of talk, people were concerned to trace the reasons that underlay action, and thus had a wide frame of reference. The interconnection of events and a relationship between provocation and retaliation were possibilities well understood. It was also understood that, for the purposes of making some settlement, the ramifications of an issue might have to be truncated. Nevertheless, disputants were often allowed to enlarge upon their grievances. In informal courts nowadays only a number of these will be selected for final consideration (and one may presume in the past were 'listened to'), but the actual process of 'talking out' was seen to have intrinsic value.[3] Talk revealed a disputant's attitudes and feelings, both as they were at the time of the offence and as they had become in prospect of a settlement. Criticism was voiced chiefly when, it was said, the parties began 'fighting' with speeches - ik ndip onom ('the words catch fire'). The function of talking (to reach compromise) had been lost: each side was reduced to defending its position and attacking the other just as though it were engaged in combat. For this reason too much talk was considered dangerous.

Reconciliation might be reached by disputants desiring a return to a state of affairs where their minds were free of grievances; or in their coming together to demonstrate an overt

---

[1] Further meanings of the word are found in A.J. Strathern (1972a).

[2] See pp.28-32 for the description of a case in which the pukl of a contest over garden rights was seen to stem from previous dissension over bridewealth.

[3] Cf. B.J. Brown (1969:184).

clearance of revenge motives, so that at least outward cause for conflict was removed and there was a basis (where appropriate) for a resumption of relations. Nowadays hope is expressed in public that personal animosity has been allayed. (In unofficial courts today a person who agrees to pay compensation for something he has done may be harangued by those present to the effect that 'You must not harbour a grudge because you have to pay over these items; it was your fault that led you into this situation, and the affair is now finished'. The person receiving the compensation is told in rather similar terms to be satisfied with it.) But while people hope that talking will remove popokl (resentment), they recognise that the greater the social distance between the disputants the more likely it is that public rapprochement fails to modify personal feelings.

The process by which the pukl was excavated often involved protracted argument and discussion. Big-men rose to meet the challenge to their skills. The principals would be motivated to make the most plausible defence of their situation, and some men took pride in having 'sharp talk', on which they relied to extricate themselves from incriminating situations. Disputants were regarded as likely to dissemble, bring out only half the truth, obscure issues and twist facts, and in short 'trick' those trying to get to the root of the matter. Hence the emphasis on the effort required to dig out the talk. Indeed, Hageners nowadays refer to the craftiness with which big-men themselves, perhaps playing several games, sometimes attempt to influence a dispute's outcome as 'trickery'. Pidgin trik has become incorporated into Melpa vocabulary, synonymous with kep ni ('to lie, to practice deception'). This was used both of the devices by which a person defeated the purpose of the confrontation, and of crimes or vengeance successfully accomplished without detection. Sometimes vengeance followed an unfavourable confrontation. Simple refusal to say anything at all came under the same rubric. (Conspirators plotting a theft might first share uncooked taro among themselves; a salient property of this 'food' was its bitterness, and the men became strengthened to withstand the bitter talk others would make against them. People also sought magic to prevent an opponent's talk from going 'straight'.) A number of terms referred to talk which was hidden, concealed or otherwise covered up. Such talk did not 'go straight'.

In this kind of context factual truth became relevant. Disputants tried to trip one another up, or others interested in the outcome pointed out flaws in their presentation: demonstration of a lie was some evidence that a whole story was fabrication. The accused would also be presented with circumstantial evidence or eye-witness accounts. There were traditional procedures by which a person under duress could prove the veracity of his own statements or challenge the veracity of others. Oaths were taken on the divination-substance (mi) of the person's own tribe: if he were lying the mi would smite him with a fatal sickness. Such drastic measures did not, however, prove single points of fact - they revealed the whole 'judicial truth':[1] whether or not the person wished the other harm and was making a true or false accusation, or was responsible for the delict in question. (Unfounded accusation could be taken as evidence of malice.)

Persuasion was not always verbal: in extreme situations physical coercion forced a person to yield recompense or made him confess. Techniques of coercion were often also acts of punishment where reconciliation had ceased to be an issue. In the past promiscuous women or poison suspects were tortured. Confession from a poisoner was crucial for future safety (her accusers would want to know from where she obtained the poison) but did not always prevent her execution. Here confession had been made too late. Women who found themselves the object of seduction or who had been handed poison should of their own accord have brought the situation into the open. The same was true when failure to reveal some delict which enraged clan ghosts brought a fatal sickness upon a man - at this late juncture talking out could not avert disaster.

Digging out talk had one important implication. The ideal confrontation led at some point to an admission or confession, 'good talk' (ik kae petem). A thief admitted he stole from a garden; a girl admitted her intentions to leave her husband. Once this had been revealed, appropriate action could ensue. Sometimes people continued to deny their involvement in a dispute. One might suppose that this would have had a similar effect, since no wrong could be proved between the two parties. But in fact a confession was always felt to be the more satisfactory outcome. The process of talking over an issue, extracting statements about people's state of mind and making adjustments in the light of this knowledge, was more rewarding for most people involved, except the defendant and his supporters, than a successful upholding of a denial. Gluckman (1955:360) has pointed out that when Barotse judges cross-examine a defendant they appear to be making an assumption of guilt, since their questions are framed as though the respondent were lying. But the assumption is no more than an apparent one, and he suggests that the judges are well aware of the implications of their techniques. In Hagen, while it was true that big-men handling a case often assumed, simply as a technique to exhaust all possibilities, that disputants were concealing evidence, as

---

[1] See p.20.

far as a plaintiff was concerned there were often no real means[1] of satisfying him that his suspicions were unfounded.

Big-men. Big-men took pride in their ability to manipulate people through words, and interference (I use the term in a neutral way) in disputes had attractions for this reason. A modern description of a now-deceased big-man of the Elti tribe indicates some of these capacities: its theme is dominance through talk.

> X was a tultul, and his name went up, all the people and the kiap knew his name; he was a strong man but ate poison and died. He went to talk to the kiap and his talk was straight, and he could ignore the talk of the kiap too, and gave talk to all the people and himself listened to no-one. Everyone had to come to ask him. He took the law of the government and took our law as well. He listened to no-one, they had to listen to him. The kiap looked at his ways; he was a good man and many kiap, too, wept when he died. He was a friend with masta Y [an ADO]. He heard courts well: he made the talk die.

Nowadays Hageners judge a man's fitness to mediate in disputes by the quality of his 'talk'. It is a quality which they also stress in their accounts of big-men of the past. In reference to the past, when peaceful settlement through compensation was only one of a number of measures open to disputants, big-men were credited with the initiative of encouraging this rather than armed conflict. Outbreaks of fighting might be inconvenient at particular junctures, interfering with their own schemes for self-advancement (as through ceremonial exchange), and transfers of wealth (compensations) could afford occasions for self-display. They stepped in to provide the necessary compensation items or suggested how these be raised. It would be unrealistic not to mention that big-men also sometimes blatantly arranged events, including the outcome of disputes, to suit themselves. A co-big-man might receive support where a 'rubbish man' would be given none; an aggrieved big-man might intimidate an offender of less eminence into raising a larger compensation than he would otherwise have given; and if he was accused of an offence, high-handedly disregard the accusations.[2] They were also unlikely, given their general position, to make recommendations wholly devoid of political expediency. Dispute-settlements were often events in wider strategies.

---

[1] Apart from swearing on the mi, a drastic action.

[2] See pp.38-40 for some details of a modern dispute between two minor big-men, in which the more senior refused to yield his position.

Nevertheless, it is also true that the really able big-man held himself to some extent (as he saw it) beyond the petty troubles which plagued little men. He was characterised as 'peaceful' or 'cool' (Strauss and Tischner 1962:211). It was in his interest to be seen to be generous, and to be able to rise above annoyances that caused vengeance-anger in others (A.J. Strathern 1971). Such an individual tended to have wide personal networks, and thus not only be interested in a broad range of disputes but often be in a position to use his links to mediate between two sides.

Stories are told nowadays about how previous big-men would upbraid a thief (for example), saying that the owner of the stolen property felt badly about it and they must sit down and work out a settlement, and since the thief was a poor man without resources, they (the big-men) would provide the valuables for compensation. One such account ends with comments imputed to big-men of both sides to the effect that they were not responsible for the theft, it was the thieves who did it, but the thieves were inferior (mana moromen, 'down below') while they themselves were on top (okla). Not only were they inferior, but little men who constantly stole or hastily got into fights or otherwise caused trouble were anit-social: ik na pitimin ('do not listen to what is said', primarily that is, to the recommendations of big-men).

One motive attributed to big-men who made such payments was the desire to turn aside criticism that the thief's whole group was without wealth. Their general prominence in local affairs lent weight to their suggestions, and it was from their mouths that the most trenchant reminders of norms and precepts would come. Kinship relations, clan membership and alliances between groups were all supported by norms of co-operation which could be brought into play. The presence of big-men might also save face: individuals wishing to retreat from their defences would point to the force of the leader's admonishments.

Legal scholars have argued whether it is appropriate to use the term 'arbitration' for such attempts at reconciliation, where a decision was binding only insofar as it proved acceptable to the parties in dispute, or whether to reserve it for situations, as in English law, where an award is seen as binding on the parties by prior agreement.[1] There was no standard way in which Hagen disputants would show submission to a big-man's recommendations, but willingness to come to some solution was a premise on which peaceful (as opposed to violent) confrontation was based. Big-men at different times acted as simple mediators, as active

---

[1] See Ollennu (1969).

negotiators, or as judges who would pronounce what they considered a proper settlement should be. In the last-mentioned circumstance they might make overt as well as covert attempts to impose their own point of view.

It is as well to stress that the intervention of such persons in disputes was by no means automatic. Many issues could be settled (or shelved) by the parties directly concerned. These might include quarrels between spouses, or affines, incest among kin, and minor thefts. It was the point at which retaliation was most likely to involve force or otherwise become a political issue that big-men would feel they could not afford to ignore the matter.

Payments. Several references have been made to the paying of compensation. This was always regarded as an alternative to retribution by force for the majority of disputes. In practice, it was seen to be an advantage between allied clans or persons linked in a friendly way, while within the clan or between close cognates it could be mandatory. I summarise certain salient points.

Payments fell into two main categories: (i) restitution, where amounts equivalent to the value of a stolen item, damage to property or a previous debt, were returned; and (ii) what I term reconciliation payments, which were paid where the injury had no cost in material terms but where a breach of norms had to be recognised or relationships brought back to some equilibrium. Adultery, incest, quarrelling and offensive behaviour such as assault fell into this category. This was so even where the protagonists were previously strangers, as could be the case in adultery suits. The wrong could not be made good again, but payment to the injured husband by the adulterer recognised that his rights had been violated. Equilibrium was restored in that he and the husband needed to have no future interest in each other's affairs. Where restitution was demanded, reconciliation items might be added to the original amount. Thus, after the theft of a pig, the thief would return a similar pig (kumøp, 'restitution') and then a further article 'to shake hands' (ki titimbil) with the owner.

'Reconciliation' is perhaps not the best term to use where a person had to be cajoled, pleaded with, perhaps even brow-beaten, into raising a 'generous' compensation. But the handing over of the items was taken as a general admission of who had the right in the matter and an acknowledgment that a modus vivendi should be found. A limit was imposed on people's requests, for they recognised that forcing too 'generous' a compensation from someone might only build up his resentment which would find outlet later.

Where quarrels were followed by a mutual desire to patch up differences, payments frequently took the form of a reciprocal exchange; for adultery, assault, theft and pollution offences they were usually unilateral. In either situation, a person agreeing to provide payment appeared to be admitting his fault (or the fault of the person for whom he was liable, as when a husband paid for a wife's delicts), though afterwards he might phrase his actions differently, pleading that he was sorry for so-and-so and wanted to end the trouble, so he made the payment although he was not really to blame.

There was no specific point in compensation-debates at which a disputant was pronounced to have done wrong. During discussion people simply aired their views that a person had been at fault on such-and-such a point. A number of terms existed for this. Klawa enem referred to a 'mistake', either a moral or technical slip; in self-reproach for giving himself away a defendant would admit to 'stupidity' (klawa). Elemnga kongon ('his work') implied that the person had brought trouble on himself, namely the predicament which had forced him to pay compensation. A similar imputation was made in mong titim ('he catches trouble'). Mong embraced both the deeds and the trouble which was their consequence. These were all quite separate from the judgment that a person had behaved badly (as is connoted in the English term 'guilt'). Kinds of behaviour referred to as 'bad' (kit) included failure to make a confession or flagrant anti-social acts such as persistent adultery or thieving - traits which appeared to be ineradicable.[1]

The aggrieved party received a measure of punitive satisfaction in extracting compensation. Sometimes it was extracted with the explicit intention that the wrong-doer should learn where his actions were likely to lead and suffer from his loss of assets. Thus a young man's elders might seize his valuables or prevent his access to other wealth (e.g., bridewealth) in order to 'make him feel'. Acts of revenge involving taking property from enemies by force would have similar motives. In these senses one can refer to the 'imposition' of a compensation, although this was never a matter of anyone accepting authoritative adjudication. The more equal in status the disputants, the more likely that settlement would be open to bargaining and negotiation. What actually persuaded a person to part with valuables varied from context to context.

Shame played a large part in intraclan delicts, especially sexual ones; a simple desire to resume normal relations might

---

[1] This greatly simplifies the issue. Actions for which a person should feel ashamed (pipil), e.g., incest, might be labelled as 'bad'. Pund titim could be used analogously to mong titim. In transactions pund is something owing, a debt.

be foremost; often a motive of generosity was involved - a thief's chagrin or embarrassment at discovery could to some extent be allayed by the magnificence of his compensation, from which he might actually gain some prestige (it was the man who could not afford to commit crimes who became the butt of scorn and invective). A threat of force might be effective between allies/minor enemies, and there was a regular procedure for staging such claims: the affronted party, along with clan supporters, would travel to the offender's settlement and assemble on a path leading to it, where they would light a fire. This was a sign that they had come for settlement, and they would sit round the fire until a response was forthcoming. In case no compensation was offered, they would be armed for attack, the fire not being extinguished until one or the other outcome eventuated.

When the successful conclusion of a claim for compensation had been achieved through the support of others, the plaintiff sometimes killed a pig which was shared among the helpers, and often between men on both sides who had been instrumental in the settlement. Typically this pig came from the compensation items which the defendant provided, for emphatic support was usually given only in important disputes, and these were also ones which merited items as large as pigs. A pig was the standard amount claimed for adultery, assault between husband and wife, and major thefts. Compensation could also be paid in shell valuables, and for minor issues in small goods such as netbags, tools and personal ornaments. Homicide was settled by large-scale intergroup payments which over time took a moka (ceremonial exchange) form. While it is true that the prospect of eating another man's pig sometimes led to plans to trick a person into committing (say) adultery, it was also true that the chance of sharing pork might encourage bystanders to press for a peaceful settlement. Theoretically it was always up to the person to allocate his compensation as he pleased, because he was showing his gratitude for the 'talk' his supporters made. It is arguable, also, that the sharing of these items indicated that the successful plaintiff had appealed to certain norms of conduct which gave him some measure of public justification. The wrong-doer himself was sometimes persuaded to hand over an extra pig for the assembly to eat.

In many cases,[1] the person providing the compensation pig would not himself share in it, although there was no general taboo, as in other parts of Papua New Guinea, on eating one's own animals. The gesture towards reconciliation was contained in the handing over of wealth; depending on circumstances, the donor

---

[1] Sacrifices might accompany the clearance of anger (popokl) from persons closely related, and here both parties would join in the meal.

was described as feeling too ashamed or too 'bad', perhaps even resentful, about the whole affair to be able to sit down and eat with the others.

In summary, the concept of reconciliation ('to make feelings good', as Hageners say) was particularly appropriate to the resolution of disturbances among closely related persons in frequent contact with one another. Co-operative relationships had to depend to some extent on amicable dispositions. In these situations peaceable agreement also allowed the person paying compensation to recover some esteem for himself. However, adjustments were also made between disputing parties which did no more than establish a basis for continuing the relationship, although outsiders might express the hope that personal feelings would also be transformed. Sometimes the punitive element, present in all compensations, dominated an aggrieved man's motives in securing payment. In unilateral payments, the recipient 'felt good' explicitly at the expense of the other. But whatever personal feelings of vengeance there were, the transfer of compensation goods was meant to block other forms of revenge: neither party would be regarded[1] as justified in taking further action, and the affair was thus 'settled'.

Modern cases

I have been describing conditions as they were 'in the past'. If it were not for the existence of detailed ethnographies from the missionary-anthropologists, Vicedom and Strauss, who were in Hagen during the early years of contact, I would be more doubtful of conclusions derived from present-day information about the past. The following disputes, which occurred during my stay at Kelua in 1970, illustrate some of the traditional principles which are still relevant to local dispute-settlement.

Case 1: the garden and the bridewealth. Territorial expansion since pacification has enabled members of tribe X to establish homesteads away from main tribal lands in good pig-pasture areas. Some individuals maintain dual residence, and there is much visiting to and fro. When the tribe was preparing during 1969 for a large dance festival to be performed in February 1970, Aiwe[2]

[1] That is, by relatively disinterested people. I am not able to do justice in this account to the sociological intricacies of public approval and disapproval. People's attitudes depended partly on their relations with the disputants, and partly on their own strategies: whether they chose to support a disputant or act in criticism or withdraw to become a spectator. Recognised norms justified any of these positions.

[2] Names are fictitious. They are taken from terms for plants, which overlap with personal names in Melpa.

and his son, Wantep, moved from the pastures back to the main settlement, allowing their houses to fall into disrepair; care of their gardens was taken over by Wømb, a youngish member of their lineage. In October 1970 Aiwe and Wantep made plans to return, but Wømb sent a message that he would stop them from living there and reassuming possession of their old gardens. He had just completed the arduous task of structural alteration and renovation to the main ditch which enclosed the cultivation area worked by himself, Aiwe and others of the lineage. He had made, single-handed, a better ditch than was ever there before, and why should the pair just walk in when it was completed to profit from his labours? Aiwe, it was true, was an old man, but his son had made no attempt to assist him.

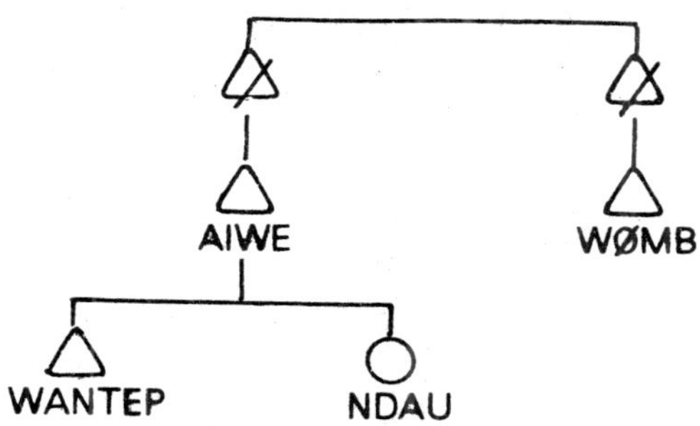

Fig. 2. Persons involved in Wømb's complaint

It was Wømb and not Aiwe who initiated discussion of the issue on census day.[1] As another hearing drew to its close, Wømb began interrupting with claims that the case of his land be heard. He wanted a particular komiti of another subclan to handle the issue, and a komiti from his own subclan agreed it was best that 'someone else' should hear the case. (As it appeared later, the chosen man was cognisant of Wømb's past history and had witnessed previous altercations to which Wømb was to refer.) The proceedings were little more than a dialogue between Wømb and the komiti. The komiti said that Wømb really had no grounds (nombokla, 'road') for a dispute.[2] Not only did Aiwe and Wantep have standing crops (including coffee) in the gardens, but Wømb possessed no right to

---

[1] Public occasions such as these, where the total population is required for assembly, often precipitate attempts to settle disputes.

[2] He later glossed this in Pidgin as i no gat trabel, i.e., there was no case.

bar them from returning to land which after all belonged to the whole tribe: lo tei na tetem ('there is no law [to do that kind of thing]'). He did, however, recognise, and commented on the fact, that Wømb was clearly angry (popokl). He could see the man was upset over the hard work invested in building the ditch and proposed that Aiwe and Wantep make a small payment to Wømb in appreciation of his work. According to his own account, Wømb accepted this and decided how they would share the garden area between them. But a week later he was back with further complaints because he had heard rumours that Aiwe was planning to bring in several Tari labourers from a nearby plantation (his daughter, Ndau, was married to one of them) to clear his section of the gardenland. This he took as an affront.

During the discussion the komiti commented not only on Wømb's present popokl state but on the fact that the energy he had put into making the massive ditch stemmed itself from Wømb's anger. This anger had its roots in arrangements made over Ndau's previous marriage. Wømb's main speech concerned this. Ik peng ile akop na nimb ent ('Now I am going to speak about the head of the matter'), he declared. The details are too complicated to record fully, but the main facts are as follows. With no immediate sisters of his own in whose bridewealth he could hope to share, Wømb decided to help Wantep raise bridewealth for a wife, which would give him prime claims on the bridewealth of Wantep's sister, Ndau. He tried to push this through before Aiwe and other senior men were ready. These men, moreover, wanted to marry Ndau off first. The upshot of several events was that Wømb was blamed for taking Ndau away from a first husband and remarrying her to a man of Y tribe who gave only a small bridewealth for her. Aiwe, Wantep and the others in fact persuaded her to leave Y so she could marry elsewhere for a larger bridewealth, and refused to return any of the valuables they owed Y; Wømb felt obliged to make good the debt, for the sake (as he put it) of good feelings between the two tribes, who were neighbours. From Ndau's final bridewealth he received no major item. His main grievance was that for all the 'help' he had given Aiwe and Wantep he had received nothing in return, and they had done a bad thing (etek kit mondoromin) in their treatment of Y. Although it was not brought up at the hearing, it was known that Wømb, a young man whose father died when he was a child, blamed Aiwe for his father's death. (Revenge was taken on his father by their enemies for an offence of Aiwe's.) It was because of his popokl that Wømb said he wanted to have nothing to do with Aiwe again, and 'put a mi' (taboo) on their co-residence.[1] These facts were the pukl (reason), Wømb insisted, for his quarrel with Aiwe.

---

[1] He had also taken a measure of revenge (self-help) by spending money which Aiwe had previously entrusted to him and then pretending

When he had finished talking the *komiti* at once raised questions about the land dispute itself; a little later he said that many of these previous troubles had already been aired in courts, and he was not going to listen to this other talk 'put on top' of the discussion over the garden. In subsequent conversation with me, the *komiti* noted that he had been thinking of how the *kiap*[1] would have handled the issue, and spoke of what would happen if the case were taken to him:

> The talk over bridewealth is different from the talk over land, this I would tell the *kiap*, and then the *kiap* would say to Wømb: 'Aiwe and Wantep can pay you for the work, but the gardens are theirs, and if you don't follow this then I'll jail you. And you can't bring in this issue of the bridewealth, that is dead'.

He (the *komiti*) added that Wømb had no case at all - the land matter was a trivial thing and the dispute over the bridewealth long since over, so he dismissed the case (*mi pilim i no inap na mi rausim dispela tok i go*).

What is interesting is that while the *komiti* was following precepts he partly attributed to the *kiap* in formulating his decision, in fact he acknowledged Wømb's state of *popokl*. He soothed him by describing the size of the ditch, praised his labour and skill, admonished Wantep for his failure to lend assistance, and was generally sympathetic. Circumstances were not conducive to speech-making. They were sitting in a tight, crushed circle, others pressing in with disputes they all wanted the *komiti* to give ear to; two yards away an altercation arose which was being settled by men of a different clan, while others were rushing by, shouting out that the *kiap* would soon be finished with his census and wanted to address the councillors and *komiti*. In spite of all this, Wømb was not cut short but was allowed to speak for as long as he wanted and on a topic with which most of his listeners must have been very familiar.

Case 2: the poison suspects. This was an incident in a series of events surrounding suspicions of poison. It illustrates some of the verbal techniques used in trying to get to the heart of a matter. Two sisters from tribe Z had made marriages, Kurup into tribe X, and Neng into tribe W. About the time of the arrival of

---

1 (continued)
it had been stolen. Interestingly enough, he reported this act to the same *komiti* whom he wanted to hear the case. It was not made public on this occasion.

[1] In this context, the full-time Local Court Magistrate.

Europeans, W had driven X from their traditional territory in a sequence of bitter and cruel hostilities. Although they had had no previous record of poisoning accusations between them, since this rout X have regarded W as prime enemies. In mid-November (1970) Kurup showed her husband a package that Neng had given her; by revealing it, Kurup implied that she was afraid it might be poison, and this was what men of X also thought. For various reasons, komiti of tribe Z were not available to discuss the matter, and X tried to arrange a confrontation with W. They supposed that a likely route for the poison would have been from W to the girl Neng, thence to Kurup, who would have been expected to introduce it into the food of the X men who shared her husband's men's house.

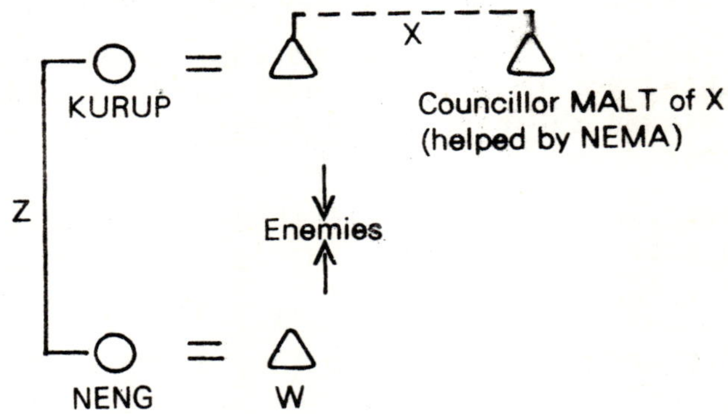

Fig. 3. Tribal affiliations of Neng, Kurup and the two councillors

Early in December a court was held in the open area between the Mt Hagen court-house and sub-district office. The chief speakers were the councillor of X, Malt, and a councillor from a neighbouring and friendly tribe, Nema. They questioned the two young women closely, and in particular asked Neng how she had come by the package. They would not credit her story that it had been found in the middle of a road. Malt cross-examined Neng on where she found it:[1]

Malt: What happened on the day you came back from a visit, tell us then -

Neng: It was coming back from there that I found the thing, as I've said.

Malt: You came and took it, then, and was it to one side of the road or the other or was it in the middle?

Neng: It was where the road went uphill, and I found it and took it, as I say.

---

[1] Translated from a tape-recording.

Malt: Whereabouts did the road go off?
Neng: To K.
Malt: Was it upstream or downstream of the K River? Where was the K main road going?
Neng: Down near the place of masta E, that's about where I got it.
Malt: Where is E [in relation to the finding place], down below or on top?
Neng: Down below a little.
Malt: That's the place of the W River bridge?
Neng: That's it, but downstream rather.
Malt: What about this masta E's house - did you take it from inside the white man's house?
Neng: It was on the road.
Malt: On the actual road! What kind of package did you pick up?
Neng: It was wrapped in polythene.
Malt: A large package or a small one?
Neng: A round package.
Malt: Well, what did you think it was?
Neng: I thought it was money that had been made into a package but when I unwrapped it and looked, it was a red thing - so thinking other people should see it I took it off.
Malt: You took it off saying others could see it, but what did you think this red thing was? This red thing, in your mind what did you think it was that you held it and took it off?
Neng: It was just a red thing which I carried off.
Malt: What was the red thing you carried off?
Neng: I thought it was nothing important[1] and carried it off.
Malt: The red thing, what did you think it was and took it off? Did you think it was paint you could use and you took it, or some cosmetic they put on their skins and you thought you'd use it and you took it, speak clearly about this, I say. Before, did your mother tell you about how she married your father and did man-magic [to prevent him from taking other wives] and you heard this and thought about it in your mind, what my mother

---

[1] Mel roltinga: 'the adjective roltinga implies that a thing is of no consequence, is easy to find, and has no secret strength attached to it, in Melpa, that it has no rondokl (strength) or pukl (basis). Poison is thought of as pre-eminently a substance which is strong, hard to discover and has a "basis" of this kind' (personal communication: A.J. Strathern).

told me about now I've found, I shall take it, and you thought it was this [magic] and took it? Now you must tell me clearly and I can hear, I say, tell me, tell me clearly, speak out, I say.

Neng: As to that, she told me nothing. It was I who just found and took off something of no significance.

Malt: Something of no significance, but what did you think it was and you took it off? People had been manufacturing new money and you thought it was some of this money that had fallen down and you saw it and picked it up, or a jacket button or something new that was lost which you discovered on the road and took to show people, or what? Tell us, inform us, speak clearly so I can understand, what did you think you'd do with it once you had picked it up? I haven't heard the bottom (pukl) of all this, I say.

Neng: It was something unimportant that I brought, I say, no-one gave it to me.

Malt: Something unimportant, no! What did you see it was, speak!

This interchange was fairly muted in tone, though Neng could not keep exasperation out of her voice at the end. The initial questioning was intended to find flaws in her story which might give a clue as to how (as Malt thought) she really did obtain the package. He concentrated on the point that she must have supposed it was something in her act of picking it up. He was mildly sarcastic in his suggestions (at a later point telling her that he and she both knew that the bundle looked nothing like an ordinary pack of paint or roll of coins). He continued pressing the same point, elaborating his suggestions, and then told her that the package was the kind of thing many people take to be poison: 'we don't make sharp talk,[1] no, the talk lies with you' (ik-e nimnga mint tetem).

Malt: This red thing, what was its appearance like, what colour was it, you saw it and you can identify it, and you can tell us the root of this, I say. Was it big or small, long or short?

Neng: A smallish lump.

Malt: A lump as big as my finger like this [indicating size] or like this?

---

[1] That is, we are not throwing accusations around for no purpose.

Neng: A lump [as so].
Malt: Was there one short lump or several?
Neng: One lump, but when I held it, it broke.
Malt: Then did you think you'd use it as paint? Did you think it was paint you could use, say!
Neng: It was a red thing, something unimportant and I picked it up.
Malt: A red thing that white women use and you thought you'd paint your lips, did you?...

Again, after this round of questions, patience was giving way to mutual signs of annoyance. The purpose of this constant driving at the same question over and again (what did she imagine she had picked up?) was intended eventually, as it was explained afterwards, to tire her with questions so that she would reveal the truth. But she held out, insisting always it was 'just something'. Councillor Nema then took over the questioning, following the question of identity a little way but then branching out quite differently.

Malt: Was it a European thing or a native thing, in a bamboo container or wrapped up, do you think?
Nema: In a bottle or a bamboo?
Neng: Wrapped up in polythene.
Nema: Polythene? What was its appearance? Was it a white thing or a red thing you took off?
Neng: A red thing.
Nema: How could your mother know what it was? [Neng had previously described how she had taken it home to show her mother.]
Neng: I took it so she could look at it.
Nema: Your mother knows about European things [lit. has turned into a stranger], she knows about European ways so you took it off to let her see it? She has experience of Europeans and handles this kind of thing [i.e., is an authority]! I am asking. You supposed your mother had seen and knew about these things, knew all about them, so you took it off - and then you showed her?
Neng: The red thing that was on the road I took off, saying that the woman could see it.
Nema: You saw it and you didn't know what it was, and how was your mother to identify it! Do you hear? This thing is to eat,[1] they say, and you come and you can hold it, they'll give it

---

[1] Poison may be referred to obliquely as 'food'. 'They' refers to the X men who were questioning her.

to you, they say, and you can eat it! Em bai yu yet kaikai [this said in Pidgin]. If the white man [i.e., kiap] says it is not something to eat, then what?[1]

Neng: Then I shall eat it and never come back [die], I myself shall eat it.

Nema: Eh?

Neng: See if I live or die!

Nema: If the kiap says it is not something to be eaten and you eat it, then suppose you die, and then what will you do? If he says you can't eat it, what will you do?

Neng: I saw something that was there and took it. [She was saying she did not think it was poison.] If he says eat it, then I can eat it and I'll die!

Nema: It would be a good thing if you ate it!

Neng: I shall eat it!

Nema: If the kiap says it is nothing[2] then you and the kiap can both eat it. If the kiap says of this thing it is just rubbish [and not poison], then you and the kiap can eat it spread with butter or something on a biscuit. If the kiap says this is a dangerous thing [i.e., is poison, lit. trouble lies there, mong petem], then are we suggesting that we should all eat it together with the W, do we talk of this? No - you can eat it alone.

Neng: Oh, I shall eat it myself!

Nema: You thought it was a native thing and showed it to your mother to identify, and your mother knows a lot so you took it off for her to have! If somebody gave it to you, speak out, and let's talk about this.

Neng: No.

Nema: You found it on the road, but if you had really thought it was nothing you would have thrown it away; you recognised it and knew what it was. Something else you would have thrown away, this was something you recognised and picked up. You can eat by yourself all right! The person who gave it to you, call his name, this is what we are talking about.

---

[1] They were thinking of taking the case to the sub-district office. He is directly suggesting it is 'something to eat', i.e., poison, but which the kiap, because it is poison, will forbid them to eat. If the kiap says they are not to eat it, that will prove it is poison, and if they give it to Neng to eat, she will die.

[2] In reference to the well-known official attitude of scepticism, i.e. if the kiap denies it is poison.

Neng: No-one gave it to me. It was on the road. I myself shall eat it.

Nema: We are talking about you dying, do you understand?

Neng: I can die!

Nema: It is the X along with V [an allied tribe] who wage war with the W. You are an eastern woman,[1] you are from somewhere else and we talk of you dying. You will die. People give wives to men in marriage, that's all: you are an eastern woman, and they have given you over here to a central man,[2] and of your relatives who could it be that gave you poison if they did this [i.e., her own folk are not implicated]! Talk clearly about these matters and let us discuss it. You are from somewhere else. You are an eastern woman and don't realise that we central people here are involved in a dispute, which is what we are talking about. Saying it was on the road you do wrong (klawa), don't do that, no, the trouble (ukl mong) is between us central X and W, over here. The W married you with bridewealth, you are just a woman given to the W, so you can call the name. Speak! Speak! The man who held the thing and gave it to you, he can eat it, and then you can have a divorce and marry someone else.

Nema left direct questioning for a number of suggestions by which he hoped to persuade Neng to reveal what he suspected was the truth. He launched first into sarcasm, pouring ridicule on her statement that she took it off just to show her mother, asking what kind of authority her mother was. (At previous discussions they had in fact debated whether to show the package to experienced Europeans for identification.) This turned into threat: if the kiap pronounced that it was inedible, that is, indeed had poisonous properties, they would make her eat it. Her nonchalance drove him to the suggestion that she could eat it even if the kiap dismissed the thing, as it was likely he would do. The councillors' threats were made with the intent of making her afraid so she would speak out. Such threats echo the kind of treatment a suspect might have received in the past during torture or slow death. One commentary from X was that the woman would have had no 'road' were it not for

---

1 Giving the name of the region where her tribe, Z, live.

2 Naming the region of W tribe.

the presence of Europeans (nau waitman i kamap ol i hambak liklik, that is, get away with behaviour which in the past would have warranted severe punishment). The same commentator said that Neng's denials were just a 'trick', although one might add that the promises to give her a divorce and remarriage also fall into the Hagen category of 'trickery': deceptions to elicit confession. Nema then became reasonable, pointing out to her that she must have had some cause to pick up the item in the first place. Reasonableness gave way to cajolery, and finally an appeal to her intelligence and loyalties. Nema told her that she had nothing to do with the quarrel between W and X, who were old enemies - her tie with the W was only one of marriage and that could be broken; there was no need for her to help the W by her concealments (the story that she found it on the road). What fundamental reason had she to side with the W? He begged her to tell them the names they wanted to hear.

Case 3: the dog and the casuarina tree. This case describes the consequences of an act of revenge.

Tokakl is an ageing big-man and a former luluai who, with no sons of his own, had helped in the upbringing of a boy of his lineage, Yuimb. Yuimb, now a minor big-man and one-time komiti, occasionally talks of himself as a successor to the big-men of Tokakl's generation. In early October one of his pigs broke into a new garden which Tokakl had been tilling, to be chased out first by the gardener himself and then by the latter's dog. Tokakl afterwards admitted that he set the dog on the animal, but added that Yuimb and several others had had many warnings about tying up their pigs away from the new gardens. Traditionally if, after warnings, a pig broke down the fence and damaged a garden, the gardener was entitled to kill the pig and would present the carcass to the pig-owner. In this case little damage had been done by the marauding animal - but Tokakl was afraid that it would learn to know its way into the garden.

The pig had been bitten and, according to Yuimb, was 'dying'. That night he came wailing in front of Tokakl's men's house on the ceremonial ground, smothered himself in ashes as a sign of grief, and in anger tore down a casuarina sapling which Tokakl had planted. This was no ordinary casuarina but one set into an ornamental tub in celebration of exchange festivals which the clan had held in 1966. Such plants (poklambo) are associated with the ancestral ghosts who oversee a clan's enterprises. Finally, Yuimb went off to report the incident to the local councillor. The next day there was considerable discussion of the affair; but it was clear that the pig was not going to die, and although there was talk of holding an unofficial court, nothing eventuated. One factor in this was the intransigence of Tokakl.

Tokakl, the ex-luluai, was annoyed that Yuimb had reported the matter to the councillor. His prime grievance was that Yuimb's revenge was an assault on his status. Didn't Yuimb realise he would be nothing without his (Tokakl's) support, wouldn't indeed the whole tribe be lost without his leadership? How could Yuimb possibly get up and make a case against him? He (Tokakl) was a big-man who made moka, brought renown to the ceremonial ground, and looked after everyone. Yuimb's presumptuousness was beyond belief. Words to this effect were spoken in the ear of the local komiti, and later during a fierce public altercation between the two protagonists.[1] To strengthen his position, he was able to condemn Yuimb's act of revenge in attacking the casuarina tree, which after all symbolised the joint successes of the clansmen. Yuimb claimed that he was just as good as Tokakl at making moka or at any other prestigious activity that could be named, and that for the latter to set his dog on his pig was an act of outright aggression. Tearing down the tree symbolised Yuimb's own feelings: he felt that Tokakl had attacked the heart of their relationship, and the dying tree was to indicate to Tokakl that he had overstepped the mark. Hence his denial that the latter was in any way 'superior' to him. To me, Yuimb privately explained there were three points involved: pigs are used to buy bridewealth for the sons of the lineage, and Totakl, in attacking Yuimb's pig, was making an attack on the future prosperity of their joint descendants; more directly, by inflicting injury on the pig, Tokakl was injuring Yuimb; finally, Yuimb was Tokakl's successor, and in effect the luluai was attacking himself. Yuimb corresponding attack on the tree was first to injure the tree as his pig had been injured; secondly, to strike at Tokakl as Tokakl had struck at him; and thirdly, since he was Tokakl's successor and thus a source of the old man's future 'life', or 'growth', by striking something which symbolised Tokakl's 'life' (the tree)[2] he would bring home to him that Tokakl had been injuring himself. Such at least were his motives for this act of revenge, as a result of the hurt Tokakl had done to their relationship.

Public opinion took neither side. In damaging the casuarina, Yuimb had also damaged public property. For this he was roundly criticised. It was also recognised that his act had blown up

---

[1] Carried away at one point, Yuimb threatened to leave, abandoning his house and gardens to neighbours from another tribe and taking with him the bones of a long-dead son that had been reposing in the clan cemetery.

[2] An equation is often made between the growing trees a person has planted and his own life.

the whole issue: restricted to the garden dispute, the affair could have been settled by some small compensation arrangement; but now there were 'two competing talks' (ik ponmbil)[1] - two parallel cases - the pig of Yuimb and the tree of Tokakl. It was also well known that Tokakl was unlikely to respond to any simple solution, and this intransigence itself came under criticism. Such indeed proved to be the case. Whereas Yuimb seemed anxious for settlement, Tokakl would have nothing to do with procedures proposed. An ex-tultul of their clan suggested that the pair exchange gifts and pool money with which they could buy frozen meat (an alternative to pork; in the past they would have made a small sacrifice). In the end, Yuimb produced some money to buy rice and tinned meat. This he shared with others of his clan, as an atonement for his attack on corporate property. Yuimb then removed the now dried and shrivelled sapling. He said now his anger was over and he felt better. But far from responding to Yuimb's offer to 'shake hands', Tokakl actually put back the tree, propping it up for all to see as a public reminder of his still active grievance. Subsequently Tokakl tried to hold a court over his tree with the councillor and two local komiti. All three men refused to have anything to do with the case: it was his fault for not having agreed to reconciliation earlier. (Tokakl had also previously said he wanted to have nothing to do with councillors or komiti but would go straight to a kiap, and rationalised this by saying that the ceremonial ground with its trees is a place kiap 'know about' for census is held and taxes are collected there.) Moreover, they pointed out that Tokakl did not own the ceremonial ground; it belonged to Tokakl and Yuimb and everyone there alike, and how could they hear a court? It was up to Tokakl and Yuimb to be reconciled to each other.

Case 4: the incident of the knotted string. Kwang and his wife, Kuklnga, were in their coffee garden; wanting a cigarette, Kwang left off work and rummaged about in his wife's netbag. He came across a piece of string in which nine knots had been tied. His suspicion was aroused, for tallies like these are kept when a person wishes to record grievances for purposes of vengeance. A quarrel blew up, and in the presence of a komiti and later a councillor the 'talk came out'. Kuklnga revealed that indeed she had precisely nine grievances against her husband. Most of them were to do with alleged debts owing to her kin. She denied that she had any ulterior purpose and said she had just wanted to keep a record in case the debts were not made good. The komiti grumbled at this secretive measure, which was just like keeping things bottled up in one's noman (mind); the proper course would have been

---

[1] A variant of the term given in A.M. Strathern (1972:170).

to report grievances to the komiti so that he would have foreknowledge if the issues did indeed ever warrant a court hearing. As it was, she was harbouring anger (popokl) and this was having harmful effects. Combined with the husband's own anger (on a number of other points), it was the cause of a sickness from which Kwang had been suffering for a long time. They were both to come clean with their 'talk', and Kwang would recover. The councillor said that there was a little wrong on both sides: Kwang in allowing the debts to build up and Kuklnga in hiding her grievances. For knotting up her mind in anger, the woman was told to find a small pig.[1] They would kill and eat it, along with councillor, komiti and others, and both husband and wife would make a full confession, the rope being burnt in a fire. Then there would be no more anger (popokl) between husband and wife.

Among the grievances Kuklnga had was annoyance with her husband for accusing her of philandering with one of his clan brothers. His suspicions, she claimed, were groundless. This same man happened to be childless, and Kwang and Kuklnga had previously agreed to let him adopt their youngest daughter when she was weaned. Kwang mistook a tin of meat he brought for this child as a gift for his wife. The brother was hurt by Kwang's apparent accusation (it was not made to his face), and stopped playing with the child or bringing her titbits. After a while, things were patched up. This was done without reference to any councillor or komiti. Kwang sent a message for the brother to come, made it clear that he was sad at the loss of friendship, and indicated that he really wanted the man to look after his daughter. In return, the brother gave him $3, and the affair was regarded as closed. Both declared they would be friends again and to all appearances resumed amicable relations.

Here we see attitudes towards 'hiding talk', and a dispute being settled first in the presence of councillors and komiti and then privately.

---

1 The chronic ailments of her husband put the onus on her.

Chapter 2

The official judicial structure

> *Kiap* Taylor came to Kelua and I rounded on patrol with him and gave law to everyone. (A former Penambe *luluai*)

> *Anda-nt lo bikhet em wete lo bikhet etemba e-nga nombokla ti mon*: the old man bigheads with the law [refuses to come to an unofficial court], but there is no road for bigheading with the law [for not abiding by the rule of law]. (*Komiti* criticising a defendant for not coming to an unofficial court hearing)

Establishing control, 1933 to the 1950s

European explorers entered the Hagen region in 1933. They travelled along the broad Wahgi Valley, where Hageners say they used to see spirit fires burning at night. Their early fears about Europeans themselves being spirits did not survive close acquaintance. Hageners accompanied exploratory patrols made from the camps at Kelua[1] and Mokei, and subsequently participated in the pacification of outlying areas. During the Pacific war there were at least eight Hagen police recruits on a training scheme at Rabaul.

Although Hagen became a base for explorations and attracted missionaries from as early as 1934, consolidation of government influence through the establishment of a regular patrol post was not made until early 1938. The new post fell within the boundaries of the Madang District. The area remained uncontrolled until after the war, but by 1939 partial government influence had extended to a ten-mile radius of the post, within which 22,000 people had been counted during census patrols.[2] As soon as civil

---

[1] Kelua no.2, the old 'Hagen landing ground' (Leahy and Crain 1937). Airstrips were established at both camps, and by the Lutheran mission at Ogelbeng. The Mokei strip became the site of the present Mt Hagen township.

[2] *Report to the Council of the League of Nations on the Administration of the Territory of New Guinea, 1939-40* (1941:26-7).

administration was resumed, a new Central Highlands District was created, of which Hagen formed a sub-district. Mt Hagen subsequently became the headquarters of the present Western Highlands District. The end of the war brought with it systematic pacification, which by the early 1950s encompassed almost the entire sub-district.

Pacification meant first and foremost the ending of large-scale warfare. It also meant discouraging any kind of tendency towards fighting, and settlement of disputes by Administration personnel was one crucial means by which government influence was extended.[1] An early report states: 'Tribal disputes still occur, but these are speedily adjusted by the officer in charge'.[2] The following year it is noted: '...the endeavour is to develop headmen to assist in the task of administration, and experience during the year indicated that success with the various groups largely depends on the headmen...'.[3]

Elsewhere in the controlled parts of the country the Administration had been appointing _luluai_ and _tultul_, who were responsible for good order at the village level.[4] _Luluai_ were encouraged to assist in the adjustment of village matters. These officials do not appear in reports of patrols made out from Mt Hagen until after 1950. The first appointments in Hagen were of headmen, known locally as _bosboi_. One pre-war appointee described his encounter with the _kiap_ as follows: everyone else, he said, was terrified of them; he alone had the strength to approach and, more than this, talk with these men - 'so they saw my ways and marked me as a _bosboi_'. The feeling that it took an exceptional person to so link himself to the new _kiap_ may partly account for the plethora of _bosboi_ which the Administration found when regular patrols resumed in 1945. The number was so large, in fact, that it had to be reduced through demotion. Some headmen had been nominated by military authorities but others had seemingly appointed themselves or had been appointed by existing _bosboi_.[5] Such a

---

[1] See, for example, _Report to the Council of the League of Nations on the Administration of the Territory of New Guinea 1937-38_ (1939).

[2] _Report to the Council of the League of Nations on the Administration of the Territory of New Guinea 1938-39_ (1940:24).

[3] _Report to the Council of the League of Nations on the Administration of the Territory of New Guinea 1939-40_ (1941:27).

[4] For discussion of the functions of these village officials in the highlands see, for example, P. Brown (1963) and her references to earlier works, Salisbury (1964) and Reay (1964).

[5] Bulmer (1961) describes a similar situation in Kyaka, and Berndt (1962:320) in the Kainantu area.

process, as Hageners saw it, accorded with Administration policy and, by their accounts, continued after the war. Men from central Hagen describe how their headmen created *bosboi* in outlying areas. One individual recalled the names of forty-two important men whom he had 'marked' to be *bosboi*, all chosen for their 'strong talk' (*ik rondokl*). He told them that they should make roads and hear courts, and he introduced them to the *kiap* who then gave each man a cane as a symbol of office. Several interesting points here throw light on early reactions to the Administration.

Headmen from around the Mt Hagen station certainly volunteered to accompany Administration officers on their regular patrols and on patrols sent out to break up groups reported to be fighting. According to their accounts now, sometimes they went in the company of police and sometimes they themselves initiated investigation into trouble spots. They would thus be present on occasions when *bosboi* were officially appointed. In some cases they might suggest suitable candidates. Where they were left to supervise roadwork, they nominated persons to help in the organisation of labour, who would then be presented to the *kiap* for approval. From the *kiap*'s point of view, this and not the process of nomination would be the act of appointment; whereas the appointee himself might well consider that he was chosen for his merits alone and deny that other headmen had any part in his recognition by the *kiap*.

As they represent it to themselves now, many of the early headmen felt themselves to be directly involved in the Administration's 'opening up' of the Hagen region. Invariably such persons were men of some standing, who appear to have seen how the novel situation might bring them prestige. The big-man who claims to have been instrumental in making appointments is responding in the same way as the appointee who claims the office was given to him because of his personal strength and impressiveness. Both see themselves as having positions of privileged attachment to the *kiap*.

People refer to the bestowal of appointment in terms of being 'given a cane' by the *kiap*. Such marks of office preceded the badges which *luluai* and *tultul* later wore. It was an appropriate symbol: on the one hand the cane was used to thrash a notion of law into offenders, while on the other hand it replaced recourse to spears or bows and arrows. The *kiap* were supposed to beat recalcitrant criminals, and headmen (and later *luluai* and *tultul*) saw in the cane the authorisation of their own power to inflict physical punishment on those who 'did not hear their talk'. It was compared also to the *kiap*'s shotgun or his ability to put culprits into jail. With the granting of the cane, the *kiap*, it is recalled, was supposed to say:

> Do not carry weapons, only the cane! If you see others with weapons, break up their spears and bows and arrows. You must build roads. And when men fight, steal or quarrel, or kill pigs, you must hear courts; and then if they refuse to listen (Pidgin bikhet), bring them to me and I can jail them.

With the coming of the council system, it is said, the kiap put a taboo on the use of canes, as he did on physical punishment by councillors.

One Administration official denied that such canes were issued,[1] or that they were the subject of a specific ruling in 1962-63 when councils were established, although a patrol report of 1945 mentions their being carried as 'signifying government appointment'. In other words, from the earliest days Hagen leaders saw themselves as being invested with an authority which is not fully acknowledged by the Administration. This interpretation shows clearly in their attitude to 'hearing courts'. I shall try to demonstrate its positive value and its contribution to Hageners' acceptance of the whole notion of law. But first I turn to the official judicial system.

The Court of Native Affairs, 1945-66

Among instructions issued to patrol officers (kiap) in Hagen just after the war were points relating to disputes. They should endeavour to hear native complaints and make equitable settlements where possible. If matters warranted a charge under the Native Administration Regulations, persons should be brought to the station to appear before the Court of Native Affairs. The CNA was an officially constituted court of summary jurisdiction empowered to consider offences by, and also civil actions between, indigenes, as set out in the Native Administration Regulations. District officers were ex officio members of the CNA, and patrol officers could receive special authorisation as such. The CNA could be convened, when necessary, during the course of a patrol. It was replaced by the Local Court in 1966.

Hageners' initial contact with the court would thus have been through kiap, persons who were also encouraged to personally arbitrate or mediate in 'matters of simple routine' on an informal basis. Kiap in turn were told to encourage and support the

---

[1] The cane material itself came from the northern Jimi Valley; some former headmen describe how they cut lengths for themselves, others how they took lengths from the cane brought to Mt Hagen station as building material. A man who did this who was not a bosboi, it is said, would have been jailed by the kiap.

authority of recognised headmen and give approval to headmen who settled minor disputes themselves. From the official point of view, these men were mediating in out-of-court settlements just as patrolling kiap did and had no formal judicial powers. Men of eminence in the local community who informally mediated in cases were doing so simply because of their traditional standing.

Luluai were given limited police powers and were able to arrest persons suspected of offences (to bring them before the CNA), had a duty to report offences to the authorities, and could bring to court persons failing to heed their orders on certain specified matters. Tultul, and subordinates who at this period had the title of bosboi, thought of themselves as having similar duties. Direct reports were brought to the station at Mt Hagen from groups living near the township. Further away from Mt Hagen, local patrol posts were established, often under the supervision of a policeman, whose job was to implement such Administration tasks as roadbuilding, support the authority of the local village officials, and refer serious offences to the kiap.

Table 2.1 indicates the number of cases which the Court of Native Affairs heard in 1957, 1960 and 1963, just prior to and about the time that the offices of luluai and tultul were abolished and local government councillors elected. Between 1960 and 1963 three local government councils (Dei and the then Mt Hagen and Kui) were set up, although luluai and tultul still existed in some areas. For these figures, like others taken from court records in Mt Hagen, (i) units refer to number of charges (thus ten men charged with riotous behaviour means ten charges, one man charged with committing adultery with two women means two charges); (ii) I take cases over a calendar year, unlike the enumeration system of the courts (from July to June); (iii) I include all cases entered in the records kept in the registers at the court-house or at the sub-district office, although these include a minority of disputes concerning dwellers in the township, or persons on the fringes of the Hagen area (e.g., Jimi Valley, Tambul), who cannot really be considered as 'Hageners'; (iv) I am able to detail only what is recorded.

Roughly 5 per cent of the cases involved men in office, either as complainants or persons against whom complaints were made. Salisbury (1964:229) has posited that action through the CNA provided both sanctions buttressing these village officials (who could, for example, complain of disobedience to their lawful commands), and sanctions which could be used by local people against unpopular appointments (and he cites accusations of adultery brought against luluai or tultul). The same is suggested by cases

Table 2.1

Involvement of village officials in the CNA, Mt Hagen, 1957, 1960 and 1963

Year	Total no. of charges	Criminal complaints: Village official as plaintiff* For self	Criminal complaints: Village official as plaintiff* Other	Criminal complaints: Village official as defendant**	Civil complaints: Cases cited involving village officials	Total
1957	621***	11	18≠	5	3	37
1960	600	6	20	2	0	28
1963	635	1	27	0	0	28
Total	1,856	18	65	7	3	93

Source: Court of Native Affairs records.

* I have tried to distinguish (although it is not always possible to tell from the records) cases where the village official is the injured party ('for self') from cases where he is the agent reporting the matter ('other'). Charges of the former type include theft, adultery, assault, disobedience to own orders; the latter include theft, assault, riotous behaviour, obstructing CNA magistrate, disregard of order of CNA, card-playing, sorcery, spreading of rumours, indecent and offensive behaviour, misuse of fire. The distinction should not be taken too seriously: without knowing the relationships between persons involved one cannot tell whether the village official is acting directly in his own interests or not.

** Charges of adultery, failure to appear before court, spreading of rumours, abuse of office.

*** I include here, for the sake of comparability, the figure computed from the official enumeration of the cases, which was also the basis for the 1960 and 1963 figures. An examination of the 1957 cases in detail (see Table 2.2) yields a total of 648 criminal charges.

≠ Does not include one complaint brought by a medical orderly.

recorded in the Hagen court registers. It is interesting to note, moreover, that as well as successful complaints of adultery made against village officials, they themselves also brought such charges against other persons; and while there are several instances of the court upholding a village official's complaint of disobedience to his orders or of offensive or threatening behaviour to his person, there are also cases of village officials directly convicted for abuse of their office (obtaining goods unlawfully, spreading false rumours).

Encouragement of village officials to make out-of-court settlements is reflected in the 1957 conviction of a man who refused an order of his luluai to attend a meeting to discuss his alleged adultery. But also reflected is the concern that village officials should not assume unwarranted powers: the registers for 1958 record a charge brought by a police constable against two tultul who used the authority the government had conferred upon them to wrongfully attempt to extort a pig from a man in settlement of an illegal court and at the same time threaten him with exposure to the government if the pig was not produced.

The record of criminal and civil cases is combined in a single register. The proportion of civil complaints heard by the court was low (in 1957, for example, the total was six, about 1 per cent of all cases).[1] The majority of charges brought before the court were for 'criminal' offences, that is acts forbidden under the Regulations.[2]

One supposes that civil disputes were primarily the subject of out-of-court settlement. Indeed, disputes over marriage payments had to be heard out of court, and (under the Native Administration Regulations, no.133(2)) could not become a matter for civil law claims. The CNA had no official power to deal with matters relating to customary marriage. Patrol officers record that in the 1940s and 1950s outstanding debts were frequently brought to their notice to be settled informally by them. Except in the case of land demarcation, where the Administration wished to record decisions taken, a court order was not necessary if the parties to the dispute seemed agreeable to the suggested settlement. In the words of one patrol report: 'Time was set aside for the hearing

---

[1] Five land demarcation disputes and one divorce petition. There is, however, no real numerical comparability between a civil complaint and a criminal charge; in land demarcation, for example, an indefinite number of people could be involved.

[2] In this chapter I use the terms 'criminal' and 'civil' as categories of Australian law; they have no real counterparts in Hagen idiom.

of complaints. As usual these were very numerous but only a few required any court action, the rest being civil matters easily settled by an agreement when an officer is present to ensure that the matter is discussed and not fought over'.[1]

A result of this was the official tendency to categorise disputes into two types: those for which the CNA had to be convened, in effect criminal offences as defined by the Native Administration Regulations, and 'minor disputes' which could be settled out of court; the latter included troubles arising over debts, bridewealth and marriage arrangements. It is worthwhile considering the specific range of offences for which persons tended to be charged before the CNA. I take the year 1957 as an example.

Table 2.2 follows records kept of the cases. It may underestimate the number of charges initiated by officials (police or luluai/tultul) in that incumbents of an office are sometimes recorded by personal name only. Since a complaint could be laid by anyone (in a case of the CNA, any indigenous person), one may also assume that village officials were sometimes active in cases where the complaint was finally lodged as being that of a private individual or the police. It is thus not possible to use the entries in the court registers as a strict indication of the source of initiative which brings cases to court. The categories of charges are those under which the court proceeded to act, and on the part of the village officials or private individuals do not necessarily correspond to the grievances they perceived actionable.

A number of charges were concerned with the implementation of authority by the kiap, the court or village officials: failure to appear for census (140), contempt of court (33), non-compliance with orders (3), abuse of office (1), and escape from custody (1) totalled 178. Some offences were specified in Administration regulations: card-playing (27), careless use of fire (8), and drunkenness (2) totalled 37. These would not find any counterpart in traditional causes for dispute. The numerous cases of riotous behaviour (172), assault (28), and offensive behaviour (15), which totalled 215, were in line with Administration policy to discourage any recourse to physical violence, including in the out-of-court handling of disputes. Many of the offences of physical violence would have led to traditional action, as would the remaining charges, especially theft and adultery, which in all totalled 218.[2] Several of the offences in these

[1] Patrol report, Western Highlands District 127, Hagen 6-54/55.

[2] See Table 2.2, note **, concerning the inclusion of a group accusation resulting in 100 men being charged with theft.

Table 2.2

Number of criminal complaints before the CNA, Hagen sub-district, recorded by complainant, 1957

Charge	Kiap	Police	'The court'	Luluai/ tultul	Private individual	Total
Riotous behaviour	0	147	0	11	14	172
Theft	0	4*	0	2≠	136**	142
Failure to appear for census	9	0	131	0	0	140
Adultery***	0	1*	0	1≠	38	40
Contempt of court≠≠	1	22	10	0	0	33
Assault≠≠≠	0	6	0	1	21	28
Card-playing	0	27	0	0	0	27
Offensive behaviour ϕ	0	0	0	7	8	15
Spreading false reports	0	4	0	3	5	12
Indecency	0	1	0	1	7	9
Receipt of stolen goods	0	0	0	0	8	8
Careless use of fire	0	3	2	1	2	8
Sorcery	0	4	0	0	0	4
Non-compliance with orders	0	0	0	3 ϕϕ	0	3
Insult/obscenity	0	0	0	0	2	2
Drunk in public	0	2	0	0	0	2
Other ϕϕϕ	0	2	1	0	0	3
Total	10	223	144	30	241	648+

* In two cases of theft and one of adultery, the policeman himself had suffered personal loss.

** This total includes a case in which 100 men were convicted on the complaints of 37 men; 'theft', one may presume, was an accusation in the context of a dispute between two groups. If this is discounted, the total of theft charges falls to 42.

*** Includes one charge of enticement.

≠ In all three cases, the village official was the person directly suffering from theft or from adultery with his wife.

≠≠ Includes charges on the counts of giving false evidence, using abusive language to the court, failing to appear before the court, prompting witnesses.

≠≠≠ Includes charges on the counts of striking another unlawfully, unlawfully laying hold of another, using unlawful violence towards another.

ϕ Includes threatening and abusive behaviour.

ϕϕ Includes one instance of complaint by a medical orderly.

ϕϕϕ One each of abuse of office by village official ('the court'), prostitution, escape from custody (both police).

\+ There is not always clerical consistency in the numbering of charges: sometimes two related convictions appear as one case, sometimes as two. I have ignored the official numbering procedure, and tabulated total of charges.

two groups, amounting to 433, would have had some chance of out-of-court settlement before being brought to the notice of the CNA.

The most common penalty imposed by the CNA at this time (1957) was imprisonment. Of 632 criminal convictions, in only 12 cases was a fine apparently paid; very occasionally a monetary compensation was awarded to the complainant (as in two cases of adultery),[1] or restitution of property in convictions of theft, which might or might not be accompanied by a jail sentence.

The low proportion of fines in lieu of jail undoubtedly stemmed partly from the fact that there was then relatively little cash in circulation. The same explanation cannot apply to the small number of compensation awards, for here traditional valuables would presumably have proved acceptable. One may suppose that this was not felt to be an area with which the CNA should be primarily concerned. Much of its work, indeed, involved 'offences against public order', which included obscene, threatening, indecent, offensive, and riotous behaviour. And although assault is listed in The Criminal Code as an 'offence against the person', it was the use of force rather than the fact of injury which was first and foremost taken into account. While the Regulations allowed restitution for theft and arson, they did not admit that compensation could be payable for assault, or for adultery or other sexual offences. Suits for compensation because of injury could not even become civil complaints, because forbidden acts were excluded from civil claims.

The CNA did not, of course, act in isolation. It was the only court, however, whose jurisdiction was defined as relating solely to native matters. The District Court could handle issues involving indigenes but under a very differently based jurisdiction and one which applied to Europeans as well (in respect, for example, of The Criminal Code or Police Offences Ordinance). The District Court was convened only for the most serious matters, or for situations in which Europeans were involved. In 1957 it heard 35 criminal cases, all dealing with indigenes. Two convictions (for theft from Europeans) were made by the District Court, persons under other charges (31 homicide or attempted homicide, 1 rape of a girl under-age, and 1 theft of a large sum of money from a <u>tultul</u>) being committed for trial at the Supreme Court.

---

[1] Actually the Native Administration Regulations (no.84) specified penalties of fine and jail only (not compensation) for adultery.

The Local Court and the present courts system, 1966 to the 1970s

Changes in the Hagen area in the 1960s included the replacement of appointed *luluai* and *tultul* by elected councillors,[1] and withdrawal of isolated constables from police out-posts, along with the development of a regular police force. In the same decade the CNA was superseded by the Local Court. Some relevant dates are given in Table 2.3.

Table 2.3

Some changes in administration within Hagen sub-district

Dates	Village officials	Courts	Police
1945	Headmen (*bosboi*)	Court of Native	Field Constabulary (*kiap*) and out-stations under police supervision (Native Constabulary)
1950	*Luluai*, *tultul* and subordinate *bosboi*		
1961	First local govt council, Mt Hagen Kui (1962) Dei (1963) Mul (1964) Mt Hagen and Kui (1964)		Regular police in Mt Hagen town; police gradually withdrawn from out-stations
1966		Local Court	Abolition of Native Constabulary
1967		Full-time District Court Magistrate with Local Court powers	
1968	Mt Hagen Council enlarged		
1969		First indigenous Local Court Magistrate	Rural police stations (Regular Constabulary)

[1] Not that their positions are entirely analogous; some differences will be noted later.

The introduction of the Local Court[1] ended the distinction which had existed between a court dealing solely with indigenes (the CNA) and further courts (District and Supreme Courts) which had jurisdiction over non-indigenes as well. Now all three courts apply to all persons in the country. There are other bodies with special jurisdiction, for example, children's courts and warden's courts, and a higher court of appeal (Full Court), but I am not concerned with these. The three courts differ in scope, as is indicated in the scale of penalties which they may administer. Local Courts have civil jurisdiction over matters involving up to $200, including affairs regulated by native custom, and criminal jurisdiction over minor offences for which the penalties are not greater than a fine of $100 or six months' imprisonment. In the District Court a Stipendiary Magistrate has civil jurisdiction which covers claims of amounts up to $2,000, Resident and Reserve Magistrates over claims of amounts up to $1,000. The criminal jurisdiction of the District Court extends to offences punishable by up to twelve months' imprisonment or a fine of $200 or both. The Supreme Court's jurisdiction is unlimited in criminal and civil matters. Appeals from both the Local and District Courts may be made to the Supreme Court. Certain specific matters are precluded from the jurisdiction of these two lower courts, of which mention may be made of proceedings for divorce under the 1963 Marriage Ordinance.[2]

Procedure is modelled on that of Australian courts with some modification. The <u>Native Customs (Recognition) Ordinance</u> 1963 provides for the recognition of custom and its pleading and enforcement in all courts. Also all magistrates may mediate in civil matters. In issues concerning indigenes this is most likely to be done by a person in his capacity as Local Court Magistrate and the Local Court is empowered to make a decision in respect of a mediated settlement without formally rehearing the case. This means that the Local Court can ratify an agreement without demanding that it be reached through specific court procedures. Values, events and customs relevant to the local situation of the disputants can then be taken into account during the process of mediation, though they might not comprise admissible evidence in court. Mediation, an appropriate measure in civil disputes, is not applicable to criminal matters. Among offences upon which criminal charges may be laid are theft, assault, adultery and 'offensive behaviour' of various kinds: Table 2.5 provides a convenient summary of the range. Disputes which may be brought for civil mediation include marital dissension and claims for repayment of debts.

---

1 <u>Local Courts Ordinance</u> 1963-1966.

2 For other specifications, see Mattes (1969:77).

A District Court may be held by anyone with appropriate magisterial powers. As Reserve Magistrates, officers (district officer or assistant district officer) from the Division of District Administration convene such courts in the course of their general duties. They also hear Local Courts, as may their juniors (e.g., patrol officers), on special appointment.

The seat of the Supreme Court is in Port Moresby, but judges are constantly on circuit; the Supreme Court is scheduled to sit in Mt Hagen every second month. In addition to DDA officers with magisterial powers, in 1970 Hagen had two full-time magistrates. A symbol of increasing specialisation is the newly built courthouse in the town. Its formally arranged chambers contrast with the personal nature of the <u>kiap</u>'s rooms at the sub-district office. The two buildings lie, however, in close proximity, separated by some hundreds of yards but with no other major construction between them. Preliminary out-of-court meetings often take place in the intervening area, and people may feel they are offered, in some issues, a choice of magistrates.

The present Resident Magistrate, who now deals almost entirely with the District Court, has been working in Hagen on a full-time basis since 1967. He was relieved of considerable responsibility for the Local Court when the first full-time Local Court Magistrate (a New Irelander) was appointed in 1969. The present LCM is from Mekeo. Two assistant magistrates, then on probation, joined him at the end of 1970.[1]

There has been a considerable increase in Hagen, as in New Guinea as a whole,[2] in the number of cases tried before official

---

[1] Since 1970 the bench has been enlarged further. At September 1971 the complement was one Magistrate (the only expatriate) sitting full-time on the District Court, one full-time Magistrate with both District and Local Court functions, and two full-time Local Court Magistrates.

[2] Total number of cases heard (in figures given for the Local and District Courts, the number of cases tried in their civil jurisdiction is not shown; most of these would derive from criminal charges):

Court	1963-64	1964-65	1965-66	1966-67	1967-68	1968-69	1969-70	1970-71
District Court	2,020	2,289	8,013	4,056	14,233	9,829	10,799	14,802
CNA and Local Court	11,519	12,016	15,399	10,754	19,031	23,508	22,029	32,464

Source: <u>Territory of New Guinea Reports</u> (1963-64 to 1969-70) and <u>Papua New Guinea Report</u> (1970-71).

courts. Figures for Hagen remained fairly low until 1966-67, after which there was a steep rise (see Table 2.4).

Table 2.4

Civil and criminal charges heard by courts in Hagen sub-district, 1967 and 1970

Court	1967	1970*
District Court	1,120	940
Local Court	1,368	2,113

*Actually October 1969 to September 1970, inclusive. For the year 1970-71 the LCM estimates that he alone heard 2,875 police cases (personal communication), which suggests that the rate is still rising.

Table 2.4 gives some indication of the volume of cases, which may be compared with those of a decade earlier (about 600 per annum, see Table 2.1). Pressure on the Local Court in particular seems to be progressively increasing. The present LCM himself heard perhaps 1,000 cases in his first six months of office. Between July and December 1970 over 1,600 entries had been made in the Local Court registers. The records include courts convened by Administration officers, but since the appointment of the full-time LCM the majority of Local Court cases have been passing through his hands. In 1970 he was dealing with about 75 per cent of all Local Court charges. There has also been a great leap in the number of cases filed for the District Court from the 35 recorded for 1957.

Several factors relate to this increase. A crucial one has probably been the growth of judicial facilities, which has coincided also with expansion in police activity. Hageners themselves are making use of these services, especially through the police as agents to whom complaints are often initially brought. This applies most to people living within (say) a 10-to-15-mile radius of the town. The siting of the court-house in Mt Hagen, along with regular policing of the town, also means that problems peculiar to the growing township are increasingly channelled through the courts. The urban population is expanding: according to the 1966 census, there were 2,764 indigenous and 551 non-indigenous residents; in 1971, 8,398 indigenous and 1,211 non-indigenous residents (Bureau of Statistics 1972). One would expect to find charges arising from the need to maintain order within the town (such as drunkenness in public, or disorderly behaviour), and from other aspects of urban life (such as traffic offences, thefts from shops). The physical presence of the police brings further grounds for offence - obstructing an officer in the course of his duty, and so on; and by being on the spot police are able, in the interests of maintaining public order, to bring to court persons involved in brawling and quarrelling offences of the kind which in the past would never have reached the ears of a kiap.

Among charges brought before the District Court in 1970, serious thefts were a large category, as they always had been. Thefts from stores or commercial enterprises in general reflect the growth in commerce and increasing needs for cash; related to this are charges on grounds of breaking and entering or being without lawful excuse on another's premises. Other criminal charges were traffic offences, possession of unlicensed firearms, drunkenness, use of obscene language, and riotous or violent behaviour. In some cases the scale of the offence brought it before the District rather than the Local Court; in other cases the defendants chose to go to the higher court. Civil cases before the District Court included defaulting on contracts or payments. The latter covers payments for goods, for car repairs, for services provided by the Administration such as hospital fees or domestic electricity, and applies in the main to the urban community (Europeans and migrants from elsewhere in Papua New Guinea). The District Court also held preliminary hearings of charges for which the defendants were committed to trial before the Supreme Court; these included theft, acting under false pretences, some sexual offences, and wilful and attempted murder or wounding.

I examine the range of charges brought before the Local Court in Hagen over two short periods of time, one in early 1967, which was after the Local Courts Ordinance had come into effect but before a full-time magistrate was appointed to deal exclusively with Local Courts, and one in 1970, following such an appointment. The first is a two-month period; the second is a run of 200 cases which are dated to within a two-month period, though they do not cover all heard over that time.[1] In Table 2.5 the first section repeats, for the sake of comparison, offences as enumerated in Table 2.2.

One European is included in the 1967 figures; they also include other persons who from their place of origin must be

---

[1] In the compilation of court registers, which are done for the sub-district at the court-house in Mt Hagen town, cases held at the court-house (i.e., before the permanent magistrates) will be entered in chronological sequence, but the sequence will be upset by the receipt of case details from kiap convening courts outside town.

Table 2.5

Number of criminal complaints before the Local Court, Hagen sub-district, recorded for short periods in 1967 and 1970

Charge	1967 period	1970 period
Riotous behaviour	39	86
Theft	41	26
Failure to appear for census	1	0
Adultery*	7	5
Contempt of court*	8	0
Assault*	55	15
Card-playing**	43	8
Offensive behaviour	18	3
Spreading false reports	6	2
Indecency	13	0
Receipt of stolen goods	5	0
Careless use of fire	0	0
Sorcery	1	0
Non-compliance with orders	0	0
Insult/obscenity	6	1
Drunk in public	30	20
Abuse of office	2	0
Prostitution	0	0
Escape from custody	14***	2
Without lawful excuse on premises	5	10
False statement to police	2	0
Unlawfully armed	2	0
Motor offences≠	17	6
Failing to pay taxes#	(61)##	(7)##
Allowing pigs to trespass	0	2
Publicly void urine	0	2
Damage to property	1	2
Obstruct police	2	0
Without means of support	1	1
Other ϕ	2	2
Total	321	193

* Including offences as listed in Table 2.2.

** And other gambling.

*** Including 'escape' of patients from Hansenide colony, Togoba.

≠ Including traffic offences.

\# Local government council tax.

\## I chose the first two months of 1967, and during this time there were several charges concerning non-payment of council tax, following the collection of taxes about this time of year. The 1970 cases unfortunately refer to a different time of year (August-September) and are not comparable on this score, so are excluded from the totals.

ϕ One each of selling liquor without licence, passing false cheque, selling protected fauna, failing to maintain allotted section of road.

migrants to Hagen. These number over 25 per cent of those charged in 1967, and for the 1970 period some 18 per cent, although my figures are likely to be underestimates.[1] For 1957 the figure is about 5 per cent.

Because of lack of comparability in certain features of the information I present for 1957 and for 1967 and 1970, I do not wish to make a detailed assessment of differences in the patterns of charges. One or two gross points may be noted. The 1967 and 1970 figures suggest a rise in crimes of physical violence and a fall in offences concerned with the implementation of the authority of kiap[2] and possibly of village officials as well. We may note the new offences of 'false statement to police' and 'obstruction of police'. A fall in a category such as adultery (from approximately 6 per cent to 2 per cent of all charges) is more an indication that this traditional subject for litigation is less frequently being dealt with through the Local Court, than that it is less a matter for dispute in the population at large. Charges on the grounds of drinking in public have increased from 0.3 per cent to 9 per cent, while motor and traffic offences are quite novel. But in spite of the increase in such charges, issues brought up on the initiative of Hageners themselves remain a substantial proportion. Some broad comparisons are presented in Table 2.6.

The process by which a complaint comes before a court varies according to its nature, and also according to the kind of magistrate who eventually hears the case, and the local presence or absence of police. The main contrast is between bringing a complaint to a kiap on patrol and applying to the LCM in Mt Hagen town. In the first situation, representation by complainants can be made direct to the kiap, perhaps through councillors acting as spokesmen. In such a case, the charge is likely to be recorded as being on the information of the private individual or the councillor. Complaints of a criminal nature presented to the LCM in Mt Hagen are invariably siphoned through the police, to whom the individual or councillor first brings the case. The charge is likely to be recorded in a policeman's name.

---

[1] It is not always possible to be certain about the place-names given in the registers and I have here only extracted persons who for certain come from outside the Hagen sub-district. I exclude charges against personnel of the police force stationed in Hagen, although they may have come from elsewhere. Tax cases are excluded from the totals here.

[2] Also reflected in the fall of charges on failure to appear for census counts.

Table 2.6

Offences dealt with by CNA/Local Court and their relationship to traditional Hagen subjects for litigation, 1957, and 1967 and 1970

Year	Category of offence in respect of Regulations												Total	
	With no traditional counterpart						Aspects of which had traditional counterpart							
	Concerned with implementation of authority		Other		Sub-total		Concerned with physical violence		Other		Sub-total			
	No.	%	No.	%	No.	%	No.	%	No.	%	No.	%	No.	%
1957	178	27	37	6	215	33	215	33	218	34	433	67	648	100
1967 and 1970	31	6	132	26	163	32	216	42	135	26	351	68	514	100

More than two-thirds of the criminal complaints made over the two months of 1967 were recorded as being on the information of police (80 per cent of the total of 321, 70 per cent of the total of 382 if the tax cases are included); and more than this for the 1970 cases.[1] In gross terms we may compare these figures with those for 1957 when only about one-third of the charges were recorded via the police. Charges registered as having come from the police fall into three categories: (i) those placed on the complaints of other persons, for example, theft; (ii) those initiated by the police themselves, as is most likely in convictions for card-playing, and riotous or violent behaviour; and (iii) those initiated by the police as themselves injured persons - three-quarters of the charges laid in 1967 for offensive behaviour were on grounds of offensive behaviour towards members of the police force, and a number of charges for insulting or obscene language fall into the same category.

Roughly the same pattern of categories is revealed in the kinds of charges for which councillors[2] are recorded as complainants. I consider now the whole year 1967 (figures for 1970 were not compiled). It should be remembered that many of these cases would be ones heard by kiap in their capacity as Local Court Magistrates, although it was during this year that the present Resident Magistrate commenced Local Court duties. A total of 161 complaints were received from councillors which resulted in criminal charges. Some of them were brought up on behalf of other private individuals, including theft and indecent behaviour; some were initiated by themselves, such as card-playing and charges under council rules; and in a number the councillor himself had been offended against.

The second category accounted for the large majority of actions while the third category was very small (I noted only 4 cases). It is in charges of the second category that we see councillors and other village officials taking upon themselves 'policing' duties with respect to the law (as in reporting cases of card-playing (19)) and in respect of rules relating to local government councils. The latter include the large number of complaints about failure to carry out roadwork (82), and others to do with

---

[1] The exact figure is 95 per cent, but I do not put too much weight on this because the run of 200 cases is too small for comparison here: few reports of cases heard by kiap were received during this time.

[2] And other village officials (e.g., luluai) from outlying areas not at this time included within a council.

council tax,[1] truancy and maintaining census registers (total 8). Charges over council rules account for just under 60 per cent of all those recorded as laid by these officials. Infringements of local government council rules are classified as offences against public order. Both their capacity to make such rules and their role in dealing with infringements, contribute to the councillors' self-image as men of law.

The only criminal charge for which a private individual will invariably be recorded as complainant is adultery (Native Administration Regulations, no.84 (3) states it can only be by the spouse or - in his/her absence - near relative).

A word may be said about penalties. Imprisonment is the most frequently imposed penalty, although a court fine, or the offer of a fine as alternative to imprisonment, is made in a much larger proportion of cases than was so in 1957. Of the cases heard by the LCM in town, as many as half the convictions may result in payment of fines. Imprisonment is regarded as the more severe penalty by magistrates, and it is imposed by the present LCM particularly in cases of theft (as a deterrent against what is seen as a growing problem) and often in cases of assault or violence. Like the CNA of a decade ago, the present Local Court makes an award of compensation or restitution of property in no more than a handful of cases (5 in the two months of 1967 and 2 in the 200 cases from 1970).[2]

The number of formally recorded cases of civil action remains minute.[3] This is partly a function of limited jurisdiction (for example, debts and claims involving more than $200 must be dealt with by the District Court), and partly a result of disputes being channelled through the police, who will prosecute wherever there is information of a criminal offence. Only in the most trivial of complaints, for example, thefts of garden produce, might police decline to prosecute. The police have no interest in civil affairs (apart from issuing warrants once they have

---

[1] The majority of charges under this rubric come, however, from the council itself rather than from individual councillors. Since local government councils are civil bodies the police have no duties in respect of any summons they might issue. Only once an issue has been through court have the police power to execute warrants issued by a magistrate.

[2] An example from later in 1970 is given on p.115.

[3] As also seems to be so elsewhere. See Barnett (1969:161, 164).

been taken to court). I was able to find only one civil case[1] for the whole of 1967 (a complaint for return of bridewealth); rather more were heard in 1970, though the figure is still very low (none occurred in the run of 200 cases, but three - all for debts - were subsequently recorded as having been heard over that period, i.e., during August and September).

It is significant that this is in spite of the fact that, unlike the CNA, the Local Court can legally award compensation for injury as well as loss of property (Local Courts Ordinance, s. 19 (8)), and indeed is empowered to make an order for compensation in all criminal cases (s. 19 (1)). Revisions in the Native Administration Regulations now allow compensation to be payable in adultery suits (no. 84 (5)). Barnett (1969:171) has commented on the important nature of provisions such as these, although it would seem that in Hagen at least the Local Court's de facto emphasis on the criminal aspects of complaints makes its operation very similar to that of the CNA.[2] To take an example: the jurisdiction of the Local Court is formally differentiated from the CNA in its cognisance of customary marriage. Matters relating to this were entirely outside the province of the CNA. The Local Court has jurisdiction over matters of local custom, and in a civil capacity may award certificates of divorce and hear debt claims over bridewealth. As we shall see, however, marriage disputes continue to be settled mainly out of court.

In considering the Local Court and the kinds of offences with which it deals in Hagen, I have been able to refer to 'the court' as a single entity. However, any further description will have to take into account the variety of circumstances under which it may be convened. It was necessary to hint at this in even the briefest references to how offences are brought to the notice of the court. At this stage, therefore, it is essential to paint in some background to administration in the Hagen area.[3]

---

[1] With the exception of infringements of council rules, insofar as these are non-criminal. (Local Courts have jurisdiction over failures to comply with council rules (Local Courts Ordinance, s. 13 (1)).)

[2] Connections between governmental policy and the law, of which this seems to be an example, are likely, suggests Barnes (1969), to be most transparent in a plural society (see Moore 1970). I later indicate how the policy does injustice to the range of matters on which Hageners are often anxious to litigate.

[3] I shall confine myself to the region within which Hageners live, though this is smaller than the whole sub-district from which court records are compiled.

Kiap, policeman and magistrates

The functions of the district officer in Hagen underwent radical changes during the 1960s. This was largely the result of a considerable filling in of the 'governmental vacuum': it is no longer demanded of the district officer that he operate as the sole 'keeper of the peace, welfare officer, general adviser to the people, road-builder, magistrate, policeman and gaoler' in his area (Lynch 1969:58-9). Exactly what is required depends on where a particular kiap is stationed and what other administrative agencies are available. There is now, for instance, a welfare office in Mt Hagen town, under the Department of Social Development and Home Affairs, but this mainly serves people in the vicinity of the town, and elsewhere in the sub-district a local kiap may continue to handle welfare matters.

In late 1970 the sub-district office in Mt Hagen town had a field staff of 12, of whom 5 were regularly stationed at headquarters. The other 7 were at outlying posts; 3 (at Baiyer River and Tambul, the latter with two officers) were beyond the region inhabited by Hageners, while the remaining 4 were stationed at local government council chambers (Dei, Mul) or at council administrative centres (Angalimp, Nebilyer). These centres have been formed since the enlargement of the Mt Hagen Council, whose central chambers and offices are in the town. Three of the four officers were gazetted as magistrates, as is indicated in Table 2.7. All DDA officers may mediate in civil disputes brought to them, including junior men on patrol from headquarters, but only authorised magistrates hold Local Courts. (District Court matters are sent to Mt Hagen.) Where the kiap does not have magisterial powers, the Local Court travels on circuit. For a time its circuit included Dei and Angalimp, but in late 1970 only Angalimp was covered by the weekly visits.[1]

Sub-district officers in the town regard the LCM (and RM) as pre-empting their magisterial functions, although they still encourage people to come to them for arbitration. The sub-district office also handles land disputes and recommends action to be taken by a land demarcation committee or the Land Titles Commission.[2] For criminal matters appropriate for the Local or

[1] With the expansion of the bench noted on p.54 (footnote 1), from September 1971 there has been a more comprehensive circuit. Dei, Mul, Nebilyer and Angalimp, the main extra-urban centres, are all now visited weekly by full-time Local Court Magistrates.

[2] Although any Local Court Magistrate can issue a provisional order pending later decision by the Land Titles Commission, in effect it is likely to be a DDA magistrate who does this in Hagen (Land Titles Commission Ordinance s. 15A). Kiap can assist clans (or individuals) in their laying a claim to land.

Table 2.7

Some administrative agencies located in the Hagen region in 1970

Centre	Local government council	Police Constabulary	Division of District Adminis-tration	Department of Law
Mt Hagen town	Mt Hagen Council chambers*	Police station; police zone HQ	Sub-district HQ ADC and staff; magisterial powers	Court-house Full-time RM and LCM
Dei/Yan	Dei Council chambers	Rural police station	PO: magistrate	
Mul/Bukapena	Mul Council chambers	Rural police station	ADO: magistrate	
Nebilyer	Mt Hagen Council admin. centre	Rural police station	ADO: magistrate	
Angalimp	Mt Hagen Council admin. centre	Rural police station	APO	LCM on circuit
Elsewhere in the sub-district (8 locations)		Rural police stations		

* The regional local government officer is also stationed at Mt Hagen, but I am not concerned with administration at a level beyond the sub-district. It should also be noted that Mt Hagen is divisional headquarters for the Highlands Division of the police, and District headquarters for the Western Highlands District (DDA).

District Court, people are told to take their reports to the police. This releases the staff of the sub-district office for activities more appropriate to what they envisage as their changing role.

In the words of the then acting ADC:

> The role of the _kiap_ is mainly now what we call native administration, in other words, helping them to, and advising and educating them to, follow laws better - political education, local government education, business education, anything to help them behind the scenes.[1]

New problems arise for the local people, he continued: in business management as a result of their need to understand new financial procedures in banking, taxation, insurance, stocks and shares, and in their relations with other agencies such as the police or welfare office. He suggested that in these circumstances the _kiap_ should be someone to whom they could turn for advice and help. This is not at all inconsistent with his traditional role as informal arbiter or mediator in disputes.

Kiap posted away from the town are associated with council centres: at Dei and Mul they are council administrative advisers. Patrols out from Mt Hagen or the other centres are usually confined to periods of census-taking or elections, and provide occasions for political education talks. Among reasons for the decrease in patrolling over the 1960s has been the establishment of area administration by councils and the development of other departments. Roadbuilding, for example, is now under the supervision of local councils or, according to the class of road, the Department of Public Works. Moreover, routine maintenance of law and order is no longer a function of the sub-district office, which has ceased all formal policing activities in the town and the areas covered by Mt Hagen, Dei and Mul Councils. However, _kiap_ still have a very important role as peacemakers in disputes that threaten to flare up to political proportions, by discouraging recourse to violence and encouraging extra-judicial solutions where these seem appropriate.

In summary, the modern _kiap_'s major role in the Hagen region is as general adviser to the people: depending on circumstances he may also continue to act as welfare officer, magistrate and occasionally (as in the investigation of major political troubles)

---

1 From a taped conversation. I am grateful for permission to quote this.

keeper of the peace; any function as roadbuilder is tied to his position as council adviser, while he rarely acts as policeman or gaoler.

The Royal Papua and New Guinea Constabulary was, before 1966, divided into four branches; although there was always a Regular Constabulary engaged full-time on police duty, the bulk of police work was originally carried out in Hagen by the field staff of DDA (who formed a Field Constabulary) and the Native Constabulary. Members of the Native Constabulary policed the patrol posts and other rural centres (sites of rest-houses, etc.). In 1961 Mt Hagen township was declared a special district and brought under the control of officers of the Regular Constabulary, but not till some years later, and after the Regular Constabulary was enlarged with the abolition of the Native Constabulary as a separate branch in 1966, did their activities extend beyond the town. The major development was in 1969 when eleven rural police stations (a twelfth in 1970) were created. These cover the bulk of the sub-district. Areas still then under the Field Constabulary were Tambul, Baiyer River and the Jimi Valley, all of which fringe the Hagen region. At Dei (Yan), Mul (Bukapena), Nebilyer and Angalimp the stations are situated close to council chambers. The police handle facilities for detaining persons in custody; there is a central corrective institution at Baisu.

Police have no power to hear official courts, but their responsibilities include initial inquiry and investigation into complaints or information about offences brought to their notice, as well as making arrests. Their primary job is to sift through complaints in order to decide the appropriate authority to deal with each case. Sometimes this involves an interrogation of the complainant and the defendant-to-be in order to establish the facts. Since police have discretion in every case to decide whether to prosecute, their investigations are like preliminary trials. Civil matters such as disputes over bridewealth, adoption, care of children, debts or compensation claims they will direct to a kiap or to the welfare office in the town. If they themselves place a charge on the basis of a complaint, then the issue is taken to the nearest magistrate: at the council centres and away from the town, this is likely to be a kiap; when reports are handed in at the town police station, this will be the LCM. Sometimes they refer the matter back to the people concerned for further discussion, or recommend mediation by a person such as a councillor. On rural stations, their presence may act as a catalyst in out-of-court settlement. Thus they may assist at unofficial courts heard by councillors, or, as Hageners interpret it, in some situations 'hear' such courts themselves.

It is worth drawing attention to two points. First, the bringing of complaints to the attention of kiap and police reflects the way in which Hageners relate themselves to these authorities. The second point is that kiap, policemen and the full-time LCM all have definite roles to play in the out-of-court settlement of civil disputes.

Local Court procedure

The Department of Law's appointment of a full-time magistrate to Hagen has introduced a degree of formality into Local Court proceedings.

A defendant on a criminal charge is ushered (or escorted by police) into a court room, where he is required to stand at a particular spot between, and to one side of, the desk of the magistrate and the desk of the public prosecutor (invariably in police uniform). He may be required to remove the covering from his wig (traditional Hagen dress includes wigs which are ordinarily covered with bark-cloth or netting). After the preliminaries of identification, the first question is whether the defendant would like the Local or District (sometimes Supreme) Court to try his case. On his agreement to the Local Court, proceedings in an undefended case are conducted in approximately the following order. The defendant is asked if the complaint is true. If he admits it is, he is then asked to comment on a summary of the facts read by the prosecutor. Where the court is satisfied he is guilty as charged, he is further invited to make a statement, which he signs; and he is finally asked if there are special circumstances which might affect the sentence. (Hageners often take this as a request to comment upon the prospect of impending punishment, or even to declare their own choice between jail and fine.) He is then told of his right to appeal. In a case where he pleads not guilty, but the magistrate decides he is not admitting to the facts, and there has been no mistake, the trial is adjourned to a later date so that further evidence may be collected and witnesses notified. The police act as agents in collecting fine money or otherwise imposing the penalty.

Barnett (1969:172) mentions a difficulty with which many Local Court Magistrates must be faced: that of following formal procedural rules while making proceedings intelligible to those involved. Hearings I observed were all conducted by the one LCM in Hagen, so I can offer no comparisons of different solutions to this. His particular policy[1] is to allow the defendant to

---

[1] When an ordinary Hagener is on trial. Stricter procedure may be adopted for persons with formal education, and for Europeans, who are expected to have some knowledge of court processes.

speak as much as he wishes while giving his statement or in response to questioning. In general it is his opinion that it is better to listen to what people have to say than to use rules of procedure to limit their opportunity.[1] However, once a person has finished his statement, the magistrate may refuse to hear further substantive information. He also demands a precise answer to such questions as which court is to hear the case. The public is encouraged to listen to proceedings. Comments from them would be chargeable as contempt of court, but while the magistrate does not countenance direct interruptions, his attitude is one of tolerance and only on extreme provocation would he impose the sanction. In consciously making allowances for the fact that people may be ignorant of the workings of the court, he is careful to explain to the defendant the different jurisdictions of the courts in relation to penalties and will encourage persons to have the Local Court deal with the matter where this is in their best interests. He will interpret a plea of guilty from the general context of a defendant's remarks rather than from his response to the initial question and he may omit the invitation to give a statement on oath. If the defendant is presented with the possibility of giving sworn evidence, the distinctions are explained to him in terms of the weight which can be given to his words. Finally, the accused is told that if he wishes to appeal to the Supreme Court, he may seek the help of a kiap or the District Court Magistrate.

Effort is thus made to ensure that the process of trial means something. In imposing the penalty, the magistrate usually states why, for the particular case, it is high or low, and may accompany this with a homily on good behaviour. For example, he may point out that although X was provoked to attack Y, he should not have taken the law into his own hands but should have gone to a councillor or kiap. When the accused is a town-dweller living on his earnings, he may say that he knows the impending fine will involve a large proportion of the weekly wage.

Language is relevant to the question of intelligibility. Where the defendant speaks English or Pidgin, these are adopted and are adequate for the majority of cases which come formally before the Local Court. There was no permanent interpreter attached to the court in 1970, but persons of known local

---

[1] An attitude he shares in common with magistrates of lower courts elsewhere - Van Velsen (1969:142) quotes Archer (1956:109): '[English] magistrates normally show the greatest reluctance to cut short anyone concerned with the proceedings who desires to speak, however irrelevant or tedious his remarks...'.

standing who happened to be present were asked to serve for the duration of a case. The LCM was assisted in his out-of-court arbitrations by a local duty councillor, one of a committee set up by Mt Hagen Council, and this man frequently acted as interpreter. Interpreters are usually Pidgin- rather than English-speakers, and the magistrate will use Pidgin. In speaking Pidgin, he makes use of English terms such as 'District Court', 'right of appeal' (right long appeal), and others such as 'question' which one might regard in any case as Pidginised. He refrains from using the word 'guilty', although he will speak to the prosecutor in English, informing him of the plea which has been recorded. He may also address the prosecutor in English on technical matters (for example, why a charge is dismissed or not allowed). Kot ('court') and lo ('law') occur frequently. Some examples follow:

Kot i painim yu ('The court finds that you...')
Yu gat kot long dispela pasin ('You are charged for this act')
Yu ken baim kot ('You can pay a [court] fine')
I no gat lo long dispela ('This is not allowed')
Yu holim lo long han bilong yu ('You take [took] the law into your own hands')
Lo i no tok i orait ('The law does not allow ...')

Criminal charges to be laid by the police (plis kot) come first before the court on any day, foremost being cases where the accused has been detained in custody (commonly men charged with disorderly behaviour in the town). The morning is usually set aside for first hearings, the early afternoon for hearings of previously adjourned cases. Not until all the police cases have been dealt with is the magistrate free to listen to civil complaints. He remains in the court-room but with the formal adjournment of the court the police depart.

Complaints are usually brought on market day (Wednesday) or days towards the end of the week. There is frequently a concourse of anxious people waiting for the adjournment, who at once hurry up, pressing their claims, often with letters in their hands (from DDA or the welfare office recommending that the LCM deal with the matter) or summonses previously issued. On almost all occasions which I witnessed in 1970, the magistrate gave freely of his after-hours time, though as evening began to draw in people had to think of getting home. Most civil complaints come from outside the town. Time, in fact, is a conditioning factor in the form that their settlement takes.

Most cases are handled not as civil proceedings before the Local Court but through mediation. When they are before him, the magistrate encourages disputants to talk around the trouble, but cannot let them do so indefinitely. Often these are issues which have been discussed already and it is the function of the mediator to try to draw them to a head. The magistrate requires both sides to present their case but it is usually only the principals who speak. A councillor or komiti who has acted as representative in bringing the case to the LCM's notice is unlikely to be asked for his further opinion. The duty councillor who often acts as interpreter on these occasions may suggest points of local custom and often his own ideas about the dispute.

The process of mediation is very much less formal than a full court hearing - private individuals approach the magistrate directly, are not required to stand in any particular place or to take off their head-gear, are encouraged to speak as much as possible and even between themselves on some occasions while the magistrate just listens and the public is allowed to talk on points relating to the matter. But at the same time something of the formality of the court-house context is there - in the magistrate's attention to the principals, his cutting short of narratives which deal with events prior to the dispute in question, his interrogation of the litigants, and his occasional criticism of members of the public who interrupt. As will emerge in Chapter 3, much of this is related to the fact that cases of this kind are likely to have been handled already by councillors and are brought to the magistrate for a fresh appraisal. The magistrate as a consultant expects to organise and control the proceedings and to be accorded respect.

Many cases end with deferment (the parties are told to go away and think over the matter or the councillors are asked to reconsider the issue, only returning if they can find no solution). If not all parties are present, then the complainant is given a summons to call other persons to the magistrate at a later date. If agreement is reached, the litigants signify what their actions will be (repayment of debt and such like) and the magistrate may suggest the terms on which this should be made. If agreement is forthcoming only grudgingly, he can use the sanction of a court order.[1] In such a case the matter is recorded as having come before the Local Court and in retrospect the mediation is turned into a civil hearing.

---

[1] Refusal to comply with a court order can be charged as contempt of court if the order is other than one involving fine money, or an order for fine money may be submitted to the District Court which then issues a warrant of execution.

The purpose of out-of-court mediation is to provide an arena in which disputants are able to come to an agreement among themselves. One feature of the way in which the LCM handles this is worth a comment. At the end of a criminal case he often delivers a short homily on the relationship of this particular crime to general social conditions in Hagen (e.g., theft as a growing urban problem). Where litigants are Europeans this is likely to be omitted. In mediation, discussion of the social implications of certain acts - especially in disputes over marriage - forms a proportionately larger bulk of the proceedings. In trying to bring matters to a head, he may harangue the parties on their duties, for example, as spouses, point out where mistakes were made or what individuals can expect from one another, and underline the implications and likely consequences of particular actions.

There is thus a considerable contrast between cases brought to the LCM for mediation and criminal charges conducted in the Local Court. When cases are brought to a DDA magistrate, the contrast is likely to be much less marked. Previously complaints and offences of all kinds were reported directly (or through village officials) to the _kiap_, who, if he were an authorised magistrate, could deal with most matters of a criminal or civil nature. Now the police on rural stations screen many of these, but it is still possible for people to approach a _kiap_ over criminal as well as civil issues. (People living near the town have a reasonably clear idea of what should in the first instance be brought to the LCM and what to the police; the LCM would in any case at once refer criminal matters to the police for prior handling.)

Kiap more often have to deal with cases brought up by non-Pidgin speakers. They are assisted by regular interpreters employed by the Administration or by the local council. Cases are heard wherever is convenient - in an office or in the open. There is usually no formal seating arrangement, although the _kiap_ expects a posture of respect (the litigants should stand erect and may be asked to put their hands to their sides). Interrogation by the _kiap_ proceeds in both criminal hearings and civil mediations, but while he may take notes for his clarification in either case, only criminal matters are likely to be formally recorded. If a criminal offence has not been channelled through the police, then the _kiap_ must establish the facts of the matter and hear the account from the complainant as well as the defendant's story. The situation of two parties giving their version of what has happened may appear very similar to a mediation in which both litigants are asked to speak. Where a complaint involves a criminal offence (e.g., a quarrel during the course of which one party strikes another) then the magistrate must act on this. In a case such as claims for damage done to property through pig trespass, he may follow local rules in assessing compensation, rather than recording a criminal charge; while in clearly civil disputes he may refer the matter back to the people for further discussion before agreeing to mediation. Since one of the concerns of the *kiap* is to establish the facts, he sometimes imposes severe limits on what he wants to hear, so that there may be no specific point at which the defendant is asked if he has said all he has to say. More informal than the LCM's courts in one sense, *kiap*'s courts are often more rigid in another.

I have barely commented on how far official court procedures are understood by Hageners or what they might mean. Before this can be assessed, they must be placed in the wider context of other avenues to dispute-settlement. But we may briefly summarise some of the differences between Local Court processes and peaceful dispute-settlement of traditional Hagen society, in terms of the latter's court-like elements as identified in Chapter 1. Litigation through the Local Court is a 'speech-focused activity' (Frake 1969:156), and disputants are actively encouraged to talk out rather than fight out their differences; yet there is little place for verbal skill and none for direct dialogue between plaintiff and defendant. It is a 'big-man' who hears the case, yet one who is without general influence and who probably lacks interest in local (village) politics. And while payments (or jail, in default) often form part of the settlement, the punitive intent of court judgments far outweighs any reconciliatory considerations.

Chapter 3

Channels of 'out-of-court' settlement

> The indigene does not yet appreciate adequately that the courts are there to dispense civil remedies as well as criminal sanctions. (The Hon. Mr Justice Smithers (1963:222), formerly of Papua New Guinea)

> This [substance suspected of being poison] is something that can be identified. If the white kiap dismisses it, the white doctor can see it... the white men who work with files [departmental heads] can see it... and only if it is then dismissed, will we know truly it is nothing! (Councillor during an official poison trial)

In this chapter I consider some of the agencies to which Hageners can turn for 'out-of-court' mediation, including their own unofficial courts.

Administration and other European agencies

A number of official or semi-official bodies encourage Hageners to bring to them troubles which fall outside the main interest of the courts, as we have seen the Local Court Magistrate doing in a non-magisterial capacity.

Such disputes are incidents emptied of criminal content. Requirements for law and order are at issue in the control of criminal offences and a specialised machinery deals with them; institutions which handle civil complaints form a markedly less coherent system. Of course, the definition of what constitutes a 'civil dispute' is relatively vague: consultations with the complainant seeking advice on a 'problem' merge into mediations between disputants before a third party. Thus the business advisory office (now part of the Department of Business Development) in Mt Hagen town, which helps people in business affairs, may also find itself coping with troubles that are incipient 'disputes'. Hageners appeal to the European adviser for help in retrieving money invested in someone else's car or tradestore, and a confrontation with the other party is arranged. Or consultation for marriage guidance with the welfare officer reveals reasons for differences between the spouses on which the welfare officer gives an opinion and suggests a solution.

Many such matters tend to be classed by Europeans as social problems as well as civil actions. This has perhaps led to, or at least supports, a duplication of agencies to cope with them from a 'problem' point of view. Members of the sub-district office and welfare office frequently refer to developing urban problems in Mt Hagen town, revealed in an increasing incidence of theft, desertion of spouses, divorce and so on, which can be related to such environmental pressures as inadequate employment possibilities for a rising number of mainly youthful immigrants. The welfare office, in particular, is directly involved in efforts to reduce such problems through youth activities, a town sports club, community education courses, and investigation into improvements of squatters' housing;[1] in 1970 it proposed the setting up of a committee from Mt Hagen Council which would meet at intervals precisely to discuss 'social problems'. The welfare officer envisaged that likely topics would include marriage, divorce, women's position, and drinking in town and its effects on family life.

Casework by the welfare office brings involvement in additional problems. The time allocated to hearing these cases has to be shared with the demands of many other activities. In 1967, the year Hagen had its first full-time magistrate, a second welfare officer was also appointed.[2] Prior to this, casework dealt with adoption and maintenance orders, and referrals from the hospital or prison. With the new appointment, greater coverage of local social needs became an aim, and the bi-monthly reports show an increase in cases handled. Other departments were noted as referring their welfare problems to the office, but many were self-referred, that is, brought in on the initiative of the complainant himself or herself. From October 1969

---

[1] In late 1970, 3,500 people were estimated to be living in 750 'squatter houses'. Many of these would be migrants from outside the Hagen area.

[2] In 1970 the staff consisted of two European welfare officers, two local trainees and a local assistant. Most of the casework was done by one of the officers, to whom reference is made in the following account.

to September 1970, 149 cases were recorded in the files. Numbers fluctuated by month, according to the availability of staff: in some months 20 or 30, occasionally even more, new cases might be handled.[1] Problems presented by such cases included difficulties in marriages between migrants from different areas, and between Hageners and non-Hageners (concerning, for example, discrepant bridewealth customs, or maintenance arrangements when the husband migrates or is posted elsewhere), and difficulties arising from special mission stipulations for church marriages concerning monogamy and divorce.[2]

Cases brought to the welfare office in 1970 were not, however, restricted to those produced by factors of social change. Moreover, difficulties which an outsider sees as social problems may appear to those involved as not very different from other interpersonal disputes. What is conspicuously underemphasised in the formal courts is attention to civil complaints, and the welfare office is one of the agencies whose services Hageners tap in this area. This is in spite of the fact that the welfare officer does not regard himself as a mediator (but rather as someone who is willing to discuss a person's problems, explain points of law, offer advice and perhaps present the problem in a new light so that the person can come to a decision). Marital difficulties are a prime example of the type of case which falls outside criminal jurisdiction. It is also a type of case which has probably always been a focus for 'trouble' in Hagen life, though not in all its modern forms. According to the records, over half of all cases brought to the welfare office involve Hageners (see Table 3.1), the majority of whose inquiries concern this area of dispute (see Table 3.2).

A number of people might attend to the matter of a Hagen man or woman with a complaint relating to conjugal difficulties, bridewealth payments and so on. If the complainants live far from town,[3]

---

[1] Many cases were handled directly by one of the European welfare officers; some by his Papua New Guinean assistants. The office in this period also dealt with other 'cases', e.g., juvenile offenders, not recorded in the files. Perhaps fifty such offenders may be referred by the police in a year.

[2] Under the Marriage Ordinance which came into effect in 1965, church marriages consecrated by an authorised celebrant after this date are regarded as lawful unions which can be dissolved by no authority but the Supreme Court.

[3] Records of the town-based welfare office show a scatter of cases brought in from all over the sub-district. The extent to which the various agencies are used will depend not only on their accessibility but on the perceived personalities and competency of individual officers and the personalities and ambitions of local leaders.

Table 3.1

Origin of complainant in cases recorded by welfare office, Mt Hagen, between October 1969 and September 1970

Origin of other party where relevant	Origin of complainant			Total
	Hagen sub-district*	Other Papua New Guinea	Non-Papua New Guinea	
Hagen sub-district	72**	10	0	82
Other Papua New Guinea	9	52**	0	61
Non-Papua New Guinea	0	0	6**	6
Total	81	62	6	149

* Cases are classified by sub-district in the records; most from within Hagen sub-district involve Hageners.

** The 'other party' is only relevant in certain contexts, for example, a marital dispute, and in some of these cases there may be no 'other party'.

Table 3.2

Types of cases recorded by welfare office, Mt Hagen, between October 1969 and September 1970, where complainant is from Hagen sub-district

Marital trouble*	Rape, incest	Custody of child, adoption	Juvenile theft	Miscellaneous inquiries	Total
71	2	3	3	2	81

* The size of this category partly depends on what is included under its rubric (some custody-of-children problems have a 'marital' aspect, etc.). Here 'marital trouble' covers divorce, desertion, maintenance claims, quarrels, widow's re-marriage, absent husbands, problems of Christian marriages.

the choice is usually restricted to a kiap or policeman, or the relevant mission authorities. If they live nearer to the town, they are unlikely to go to the police station unless physical injury has been done, since it is known that the police do not deal in these matters. Experience has taught Hageners familiar with the town that the main interest of the police lies in violence, damage to property, theft and the like; whereas the kiap is the only person to whom land questions should be taken, since he arranges for land disputes to be brought before the land demarcation committee. For marital troubles the appropriate agencies would include the LCM, kiap in the sub-district office, welfare officers, and missionaries (in church marriages).[1] The LCM acts as mediator in marital (including bridewealth) cases more frequently than he does in disputes over other debts. The sub-district office will also listen to them when they are brought up. The welfare office, as mentioned, explicitly offers a marriage counselling service. Although problems related to social change feature in the cases, Hageners also seek out all these bodies for the solution of quasi-traditional problems (divorce following quarrels over debts, imputations of sexual irregularities or abandonment, recalcitrant wives or indifferent husbands, complaints over marriage payments and exchanges between affines). While the problems may be traditional, the officials provide avenues for airing them which did not exist in the past.[2]

A word should be said about missions: different missions vary in their policies. In Hagen it is particularly the Roman Catholic mission which encourages mediation of disputes by its priests. Marriage problems are a special concern to the church, whether one or both parties is a declared Catholic.

Hageners themselves may initiate approaches to all these authorities, who are often European[3] or at least from outside the Hagen area. Why do Hageners bring their domestic problems to such persons when they are certainly not required by law to do so? Here I mention two points. First, in their traditional settlement processes there were not necessarily any procedural differences between those which dealt with divorce or marital problems and those which dealt with other troubles. From the Hageners' point of view it is not inappropriate that magistrates, for example, to whom they are urged to take criminal cases should also speak with authority on civil matters. Not many Hageners are aware of the constitutional distinctions

---

[1] No doubt others are brought in from time to time, e.g., employers.

[2] See A.M. Strathern (1972) for the restricted range of circumstances in which women, for example, could initiate proceedings against their husbands.

[3] All kiap (with the exception of the ADO at Nebilyer, since transferred to Dei), the two welfare officers, and missionaries stationed in Hagen in 1970 were non-Papua New Guinean.

between criminal and civil hearings (although they are fully aware of the mechanics by which different types of cases are brought to the various agencies). To them, mediations and judicial sittings are both kot ('courts'). The same term may be used of disputes taken to missionaries and, to a lesser extent, the welfare office.[1]

Secondly, a certain amount of positive (though not always consistent) encouragement may be offered by these officials. *Kiap* invite people to bring them their cases in the interests of generally keeping the peace; the welfare office is concerned with social problems and personal hardships stemming from these; missionaries are interested in the preservation of a Christian way of life; finally, as we noted in Chapter 2, Local Court Magistrates are advised by ordinance that they may conduct out-of-court mediation in civil matters. The present Hagen LCM's emphasis on mediation to achieve reconciliation between disputants probably comes closest to a notion of dispute-settlement as such.

The referral network

These agencies are linked together, not in the same procedural fashion as are the Local, District and Supreme Courts, but rather as a network of bodies with a variety of solutions to offer. In rural areas the police may be loosely included in the network. In the town their advisory role is limited to informing people of whether their trouble is a matter for the *kiap* or whoever. Between missionary, welfare officer, *kiap* and LCM (the latter two in their non-magisterial capacities) marital disputes are frequently transferred. Debts and related complaints may be dealt with by a network which overlaps this one: for example, *kiap*, LCM and business advisory officer. For the purposes of illustration, I continue to consider marital problems and take the situation of Hageners living within easy access of the town. A Hagener (H) with such a problem can involve the interest of a succession of authorities.

He (H) may take the matter to a *kiap* (K) who refers it to the welfare office (W),

or H ⟶ M(ission) ⟶ W ⟶ LCM,
or H ⟶ LCM ⟶ W ⟶ W elsewhere,
or H ⟶ M ⟶ LCM,
and so on.

[1] I have heard the business advisory office referred to as a place where A could 'court' B over a debt. See Oram (in press) for a general reference to this phenomenon.

There are two processes here: the point at which the complaint is fed into the network (e.g., H ⟶ K, LCM), and the manner in which it is carried along the network, that is, referred from one authority to another (e.g., LCM ⟶ W). I deal with the latter process first.

Movement between the authorities is not entirely random. Some moves are unlikely to occur. Thus the welfare officer, kiap and LCM are unlikely to refer back to the missionary. Once the mission has passed on a problem it is usually out of its hands. Normally the track does not double back on itself if it becomes extended beyond two parties (e.g., W ⟶ LCM ⟶ K ⟶ W ⟶ LCM would rarely happen), although complaints may be referred back and forth between two persons (e.g., LCM ⟶ W ⟶ LCM). This occurs, for example, when a LCM refers a suit for divorce to the welfare office to see if reconciliation is possible, and if it proves not to be then the case is returned to the LCM for ratification. Problems are not handed on indefinitely, and settlement may be reached at any point of the network, that is, mediation can be carried out successfully by any of the agencies. But it can also happen that no settlement ensues, and the case is withdrawn by the disputants. Disputants also 'jump' the network. Thus an individual may go first to the LCM, but if he is not satisfied, on his own initiative he may then go to the welfare office, rather than have his case formally referred to the office by letter. In such circumstances a person may also go from such an authority to a missionary, although we have seen that this is not a move the officials themselves are likely to make. In a sense, the various agencies can act as appeals against one another in that a complaint can receive further hearing before another body (although there is, of course, no formal revocation of previous decisions or advice). Occasionally people come to the welfare office, for example, because they are dissatisfied with judgments handed down by a kiap (as in the case of a woman who has been refused recognition of divorce), or because further action is needed (e.g., when the Local Court has recognised[1] a divorce, but problems arise over custody of children). The agencies may also appeal to one another to strengthen their own decisions. In a case where a husband fails to appear before the LCM in settlement of a maintenance claim, the wife can be given a letter to take to the welfare officer, who himself may write to a kiap of the man's area to order the husband to appear for an interview.

---

[1] The Local Court is not itself empowered to divorce couples in cases of customary marriage, but may signify its recognition of the fact that this has been done according to local custom (Local Courts Ordinance, s.17).

Disputants are thus provided with a variety of authorities, who all tend to highlight different aspects of their problems. The agencies acknowledge that civil disputes are likely to be involute and complicated, with many sides to what appears to be 'the trouble'. Occasionally parties to a dispute may even capitalise on the situation by each approaching a different authority. In practical terms referral means that the disputants have to continue reassembling (usually on different days) as they present their case to different persons, and for reasons of inertia disputes may be dropped.

All this is very different indeed from the formal court system, where (i) transfer from police to Local Court to further court takes place in a highly specific context and will usually be one-way; (ii) once a case becomes the basis for criminal prosecution it cannot be withdrawn by the litigants; and (iii) a 'solution' or 'settlement' of some kind is inevitable.

How are disputes introduced into the network in the first place? Any individual can approach one of these authorities. Initially a complainant is probably told to gather together all the relevant parties before the complaint can be heard in full. The welfare office is an exception, since it treats a complainant in the first instance as someone with a grievance, and will listen to and perhaps record a person's complaints before advising that he or she bring in other parties for discussion. Representation from a single individual to a kiap or LCM also sometimes provides enough evidence for the official to furnish him with a letter to submit to another authority.

In many cases the complainant is accompanied by a local government councillor (or his komiti adjutant), and it may be the councillor who in fact 'makes' the complaint. Official agencies assume that recourse to them often comes only after effort has been made to settle the issues at home. Councillors are recognised as important local personages who will have taken a prominent part in previous attempts at mediation. The authorities are appealed to under the following conditions: (i) when a complainant's councillor or komiti refuses to handle his dispute; (ii) when he has his councillor's support and attempts are made to convene a meeting, but the other party refuses to come to a discussion; and (iii) perhaps the most common, when a councillor's mediation has failed. Several attempts may be made, and situations (i) or (ii) can follow initial mediation discussions. If a councillor or komiti has become involved in a dispute he may himself initiate the move to take it to an outside agency, either because of the prospect of further trouble on his hands or because he feels affronted by the behaviour of those who have not 'listened' to his words. A councillor, indeed, may complain directly of this, to the person he is consulting, calling so-and-so 'bigheaded' (<u>bikhet</u>).

Over a marriage dispute a councillor is most likely to go first to the LCM, although he will also approach the sub-district office if the affair has been dragging on for a long time. An individual presenting his case to the LCM or <u>kiap</u> who cannot get the full support of his councillor (e.g., if the councillor has other business to attend to) will nevertheless try to be introduced by a <u>komiti</u>. Individuals are much more likely to go by themselves to the welfare office although, during subsequent investigations by the welfare officer, councillors may be asked to attend.

The work of the welfare officer is less widely known than that of the LCM or <u>kiap</u>. Among people with some education, it is an agency to which women in particular feel free to carry complaints. Women may also approach missionaries directly. But unless they are equipped with letters from either of these two bodies, they are not so likely to make a direct representation to a <u>kiap</u> or LCM. The church and welfare office are known to have special attitudes towards women's marital problems and to support sets of values which present alternatives to certain traditional family values. They stress personal commitment and inclination, and, in the case of the church, monogamous unions. Where a complainant makes it clear that his or her church affiliations are important, the welfare office will support a church view on the matter.[1] Thus a Christian who presents herself as unhappy because her husband is thinking of taking a second wife will receive a sympathetic hearing. A woman whose troubles are recognised on traditional grounds tries to find a male spokesman and with his support go to the LCM or <u>kiap</u>.[2]

---

1 In mixed marriages (i.e., Christian and non-Christian spouses), however, the welfare officer will try to see both points of view. He recognises that it is sometimes problematical just how much meaning is to be attached to formal religious affiliation: persons nowadays deciding to solemnise their marriage in church do not always realise what this entails (a union officially dissolvable only by the Supreme Court). Part of his job in such circumstances is simply to explain the legal situation to the unsuspecting parties.

2 When a demonstrable injury has been inflicted, for which repercussions are known to be fairly automatic, women may alone take reports to the police station. Although I was not able to observe these processes for a long period, my impression is that the sub-district office and court-house are regarded as public areas in which men discuss things (to a much greater extent than the welfare office) and most women are shy about broaching issues by themselves where verbal presentation is all-important.

The missions form a partial system of their own, their domain of interest being restricted to marriages where at least one partner is a professed Christian. I know little about the way disputes are handled by missionaries. Both Lutheran and Catholic missions appoint helpers or mission-friends who act as mediators between the local congregations and the mission.[1] It is usually through these people that problems are brought to the attention of persons higher in the mission hierarchy. Roman Catholic missionary-priests themselves may hear troubles, but among Lutherans problems are usually handled by indigenous pastors or elders. Either kind of discussion may be referred to by Hageners as kot.

As in the case of councillors and komiti, the mission-helpers or friends will often themselves have attempted a resolution (kot) of the problem, or in any case will escort complainants to a higher authority. It is less likely that they will continue to accompany the complainant once the matter is out of church orbit, whereas councillors and komiti, whose prestige is more closely bound up with the satisfactory conclusion of a dispute, often continue to give such support. While missionaries, especially Catholics, encourage people to use channels of settlement within the church system, in fact marriage disputes involving Christians may also be mediated by councillors and komiti. The reverse does not hold: mission personnel have no informal jurisdiction outside church matters.

Missionaries and local kiap are the main agents to whom complaints can be brought in areas beyond the vicinity of Mt Hagen town (say, beyond a fifteen-mile radius). Either may, however, refer a complaint to the town-based welfare office. Presumably missions also refer cases to the kiap. Policemen (often from elsewhere in the country, although sometimes recruited from Hagen) are not formally encouraged to exercise mediatory influence, but on rural stations discussions may be held in their presence and they may be asked for advice. There is, however, no advisory communication between them and the kiap or missionary, and thus we cannot really speak of them as integral to the network. In weighty matters they would recommend mediation by a kiap.

Some points about the networks are illustrated in Fig.4. Table 3.3 summarises how cases are brought to one institution (the welfare office) and what happens to them subsequently.

---

[1] In the Lutheran case, these are in addition to indigenous lay religious teachers.

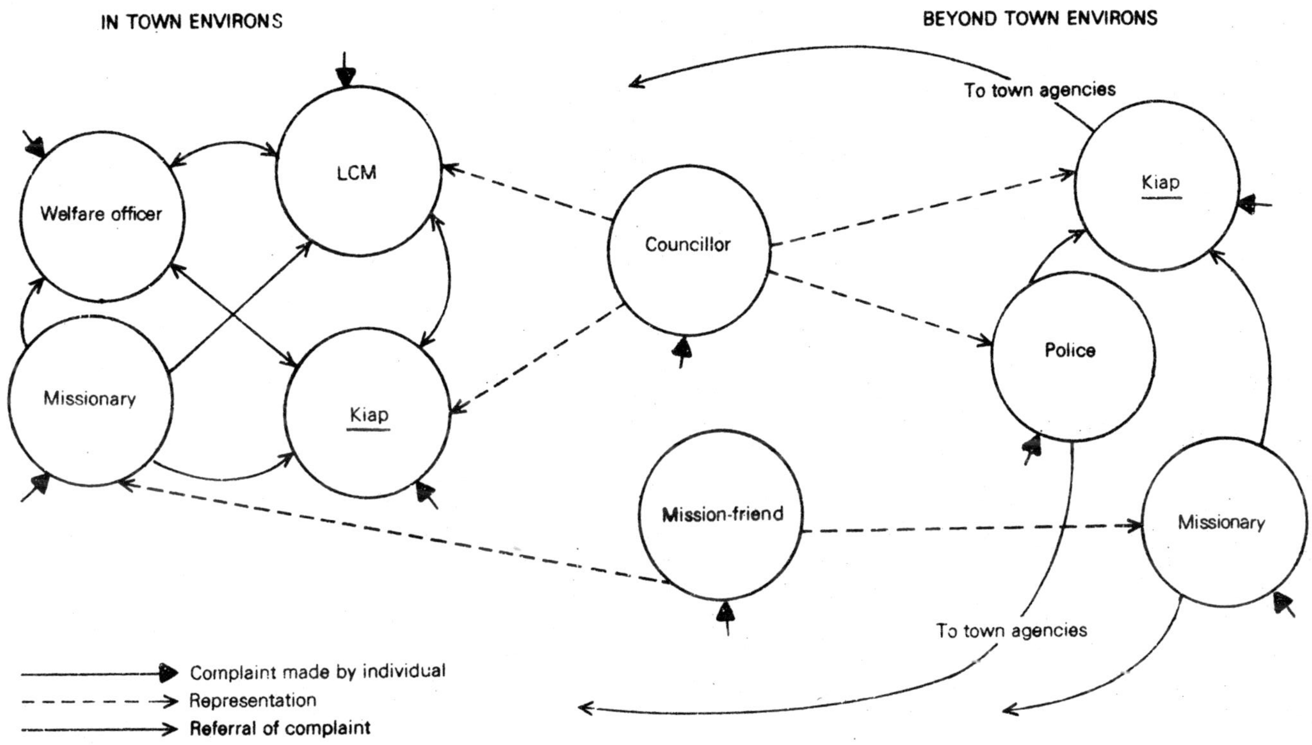

Fig. 4. Mediation networks which might be employed in civil marriage dispute

One dimension is omitted from Fig.4. In the settling of civil disputes in Hagen not only is there no overall single-way passage between the various authorities but there is no single direction in the transfer of disputes between these agencies and Hageners. At any point issues may be referred back 'to the people'; often a councillor is specifically mentioned as the person who should conduct further mediatory proceedings.[1] Sometimes the first recommendation that one of the outside agencies makes is that a dispute should go to a councillor, and this underlines the understanding that normally their mediation follows local attempts at settlement. But if someone makes a specific appeal against a councillor's decision, it will be treated in its own right. The LCM in particular is used as an agency of appeal in this way. The LCM and *kiap* stress referral to councillors more than does the welfare office, but all three will do so more than the missions, who have their own local officials.

The present LCM in Hagen makes referral to councillors (or *komiti*) an explicit part of his mediation procedure. He says that after listening to the facts of a civil case he may tell the disputants to take it outside and settle the final details with their councillors: it can be brought back to him for confirmation. 'Outside' here refers to the vicinity of the court-house (although if it is late in the day, the recommendation will be taken as advice to go home and come back if necessary at a later date). The immediate area round the court-house is flat gravel, roughly prepared, but a grassy bank rises from this, and under the shelter of trees groups of people meet to discuss their cases. Often, while 'police courts' are being heard in the court-house, local disputants will gather here and further debate their civil issues. A summons to appear before the LCM is the only effective way, in some cases, to contrive confrontation between the parties. These discussions may themselves end in settlement; a bare report of this may be carried to the LCM, or the parties may simply disperse. The duty councillor, who attended court sessions in 1970 as often as three or four days in some weeks, plays an important role in bringing disputes to a head, making further action by the LCM unnecessary. It is when no conclusion has been reached that everyone troops down to the court-house. The LCM is reluctant to deliver immediate decisions in civil complaints, and if agreement does not seem to be emerging from his discussions with the principal parties, will suggest that they all go away for further deliberation; only if no agreement is in sight after many such attempts will he adjudicate on the

---

[1] See Barnett (1967:98) for a similar situation in the Port Moresby sub-district.

Table 3.3

Referral of 81 cases concerning Hagen sub-district complainants to and by the welfare office, between October 1969 and September 1970

	Referred to welfare office by:	Referred by welfare office to (or other solution):
Self or self and sponsor	48	7
Kiap	4	4
LCM	7	3
RC mission	9	0
Welfare officer elsewhere	0	1
Police	4	1
Councillor or *komiti*	3*	2
Other**	6	0
Apparently settled by welfare officer***		20≠
Recall to welfare officer for further discussion		20≠
Outcome not known≠≠		23
Total	81	81

* There were other cases in which councillors or *komiti* accompanied the complainants, although referral was from another source.

** Leprosy control, 2; other 'village people', 2; employer, 2.

*** Settlement may, of course, take place at one of many points in the process of discussion. Table 3.3 records roughly what happened to an initial complaint. The figure here includes 11 cases where the welfare officer was apparently able to settle the issue fairly quickly himself, and 9 cases where from the records it was apparent that this took place only after further discussion with other people, and with councillors in at least two instances. (These are included in the 7 cases concerning councillors in note ≠.)

≠ In 14 of these cases involving other solutions, the welfare officer settled or was hoping to settle the issue himself but only after consultation with other agencies (as opposed to referral to them for settlement); details are: consultation with *kiap*, 4; councillors, 7; welfare officer elsewhere, 2; Mt Hagen hospital, 1. It is not always possible, however, to draw a hard line between referral to and consultation with another body.

≠≠ Some cases were still in process of being settled; in others no record appears of settlement.

affair. He can send cases back several times. He does, in his own words, encourage people as far as possible to arrive at their own solutions to their problems. The welfare officer similarly refers initial complaints back to the disputants, telling them to 'think the matter over' or 'try to adjust to each other' before returning to see him again, or to report to their councillor (see Table 3.3). This is foreshadowed in the manner in which the police siphon cases brought to them. Debt and marriage matters were cited by the police staff at one rural police station as the kinds of issues which they might recommend be taken either to the kiap or sent back to councillors for discussion.

Justification for 'sending back' cases is made on several grounds. (i) Among these agencies there is a generally accepted tenet that matters concerning local custom are best handled by the people themselves, who have a natural familiarity with them. (Local customs are treated in this way only in non-criminal contexts.) (ii) Settlement of civil matters is ideally reached through agreement between the disputants (rather than punishment of an offender) and referral between councillors and the authorities allows time for disputants to adjust to compromise or at least talk things over thoroughly. The opinion of the LCM was that everyone must be allowed to have his say and that it is important that someone invited to mediate should have an understanding of the people's problems and customs relating to these; a restricted hearing is not adequate for this kind of situation. (iii) When divorce involves customary marriage, and is the subject of complaint, by law the LCM and kiap must refer to the parties' own decision to dissolve the union before issuing a certificate which records this. They cannot themselves effect a divorce if the marriage has not been dissolved also by native custom; even less so the welfare officer, who may try to reconcile spouses but cannot take action on dissolution. (iv) A rather different reason is that the official agencies could not possibly handle all the cases that arise. Kiap have for a long time said this, and the rurally based kiap, like the welfare officer and LCM, is liable to be inundated with more disputes than he can deal with. In the kiap's case these will be mingled with criminal complaints. Encouraging people to bring in their disputes thus has to be tempered by the authorities' limited capacity to process them all. (v) There is, moreover, the feeling that it is not really the officials' business to settle 'matters of a trivial and vexatious nature'. This was particularly the attitude of the old-style, overworked kiap, who might turn marriage disputes straight over to councillors. The LCM and welfare officer, however, try to do something for everyone who comes to them and give most complaints some hearing before sending them back. Both are aware that the more matters they handle the more they will attract. (vi) *Kiap*, concerned for local political advancement, tend to voice the opinion that people must learn to dispose of small matters themselves as exercises in local government, so that referral to them is an educative process. It is also for the purpose of political education that the *kiap*, LCM and welfare officer all give open support to councillors, hoping to build up these figures as responsible-minded persons who will make fair mediators or arbiters.[1] Thus it is possible for a councillor or *komiti* to approach the LCM and request a summons to make an accused person appear at the court-house. In effect this may operate as a summons to pre-court mediations held in the court-house precincts. The LCM also listens to reports brought to him by councillors of their mediations where these have followed an initial hearing by himself.

It is clear that the councillor (and *komiti*) is a crucial figure in 'out-of-court' settlements.

Councillors and *komiti*

A councillor's most specific duty is regular attendance at monthly general meetings, at which the administration of the council area is discussed. Members also sit on committees concerned with such matters as finance, tax review, education, roads, and so on. Each councillor has a particular responsibility to his own electorate, whom he represents and to whom he should relay information about policy, discussions, plans and rules formulated by the council. The council adviser is an important figure in disseminating data and making recommendations concerning local political and economic development.

Electoral wards originally corresponded to groups of about clan size, but many have since been amalgamated. Not only was there the major amalgamation of Mt Hagen and Kui Councils in 1964, but since then attempts have been made in all councils to increase ward size where feasible. Within each ward, a councillor forms a ward committee along with two or three or more elected members, known locally as *komiti*. These committees were not, however, written into the council constitution. The use of '*komiti*' as a personal title antedated any concept of a 'committee of men'. In Hagen, *komiti* existed from the time councillors were first elected; official recognition of them has come in slow stages.

---

[1] Barnett (1969:170) interprets s.31 of the Local Courts Ordinance as encouraging influential men to participate in informal settlement.

The emergence of the *komiti* was an indigenous response to the Administration's creation of named officials in the local government councillors. Hageners perceive a direct parallel between the *luluai* or *tultul* and his subordinate *bosboi*, and the councillors and their *komiti*. In the early days men called by this title were direct appointees of the councillor. Often they came from other subgroups within the ward than that which provided the councillor himself. Thus if a councillor belonged to one of three subclans of a clan, the other two might each have their own *komiti*. It is an interesting fact that despite the enlargement of council wards, there was for some time a tendency to keep the number of *komiti* proportionate to such groupings of the population. In Mt Hagen Council in 1966-67 the 34 councillors were each assisted by an average of 6 *komiti*, whereas the average for Dei councillors was nearer 2.5. Per head of population, however, in both council areas there was one *komiti* for approximately every 150 people (156 and 147 respectively). It is only since this time that official recognition has brought with it legislation to control the number of *komiti* (Mt Hagen Council decided in 1970 to limit the number of *komiti* per councillor to four; Dei Council decided in 1968[1] that there should be one male *komiti*[2] per 100 people).

Councillors had always received a monthly salary, but in the early 1960s *komiti* had no badge of office, no duties stipulated by the council, and certainly no income. What, then, was their position? The answer gives some clues to the way the role of councillor itself is perceived.

From the viewpoint of his electors, one of the councillor's most important functions is to settle disputes.[3] This is the most significant area in which assistance was and still is required from *komiti*. There is some chance that a councillor will be a man of traditional standing,[4] although even if he is not a big-man he may be appealed to in disputes. Sometimes *komiti* become more prominent in this than the local councillor, who encourages them to deal with all they can handle before calling upon him. *Komiti* may be younger than their councillor, and

---

[1] The rule was gazetted in 1969.

[2] See p.94, footnote 1.

[3] Cf. Barnett (1969:162). Epstein (1970a:111), writing of the Tolai, says 'In the eyes of the villagers... one of the councillor's most important tasks remained the organising of hearings for the settling of disputes'. Hatanaka (1972:107) notes the prominence of Sinasina councillors and *komiti* in dealing with trouble cases.

[4] See A.J. Strathern (1970).

although some are nonentities, many have aspirations to big-man status. But why there should have to be this named office of komiti remains to be explained. A fluid situation is conceivable in which any big-man could have acted as mediator as the occasion arose, but the fact is that, although such personages will interest themselves in public affairs, it is to councillors and komiti in particular that cases are referred for deliberation.

Small domestic matters may be settled without recourse to any outsider, but traditionally others become interested in a dispute as soon as it comes into the open. Almost any fracas can escalate (quarrelling between brothers threatens clan solidarity, quarrelling between spouses brings about a confrontation of their respective clans), and it is its encouragement or prevention in which people are interested. Dispute-settlement has become a specific attribute of the councillor's role. But councillors cannot be at hand on all occasions - indeed, business or council duties increasingly make demands which take them away from their home area; this absenteeism gives rise to some complaint.[1] Moreover, where affairs in the first instance affect individuals of subgroups other than the councillor's, it may too quickly place the dispute in the public eye to call in an 'outsider', so that it is preferable to turn to someone nearer. That an office-holder (the komiti) and not just anyone is the appropriate person to whom to turn is partly a result of the relationship seen between dispute-settlement and the Administration. Given that councillors play a key role in this, others who interest themselves in dispute-settlement are tied into the councillor system as personal subordinates. Since councillors are held to derive much of their authority from the Administration, the same source of authorisation is also tapped by komiti. Komiti see themselves as adjutants of councillors (in the same way, Hageners note, as patrol officers assist district officers), and as participating in a single system of government. Finally, the abolition of luluai and tultul left a vacuum among men who were of bosboi status, and a number of the original komiti had had previous experience as bosboi. Factors which apparently limited the number of bosboi continue to be relevant: (i) only a certain number of men are interested in the position with its particular orientation to the Administration and very real workload; and (ii) on a model with the representative functions of the councillor (or village officials) it is appropriate that subordinates should represent subgroups.

---

[1] Occasionally people voice complaints that the komiti, too, are in danger of becoming so involved in government work that they do not listen to trouble cases.

From the start it appears that Hageners assumed the existence of _komiti_ was self-evident. Unofficial recognition by _kiap_ supported this. For _kiap_ accepted their bringing disputes to official notice, in the same way as councillors did, and as early as 1962 minutes of the Mt Hagen Local Government Council meetings record references made by _kiap_ to 'committees' (for example, that the councillors were not doing their job but leaving all the hard work to 'committees'). Lack of official recognition, however, meant that in their own eyes they were office-holders who worked for no reward. For a long time bitter complaints were made by _komiti_: they had to deal with a volume of casework which left them no time to plant cash crops or otherwise engage in business like their neighbours; they did not receive any income;[1] and they could not even persuade people, who would come readily to them when there was trouble to be solved, to help them with chores (fetching firewood, making gardens) as councillors were occasionally able to do.

The actual workload varies considerably from person to person, but some idea of its proportions can be given. Many court hearings last for as long as half a day, and if travelling is involved may effectively take a whole one. (Evening courts at the end of a day are rare.) In 1964 I estimated that Nip, a _komiti_ from the Dei Council area, was involved in 33 cases over a six-month period. The councillor of his clan dealt with relatively few, and Nip was a conscientious man, though by no means of high traditional standing. In that year (1964) a _komiti_ from the Mt Hagen Council area, Karingk, whose councillor was actually more active in hearing cases, became involved in 13 disputes over two months. The same _komiti_ in 1970 was concerned with 15 during one three-month period. He is perhaps the _komiti_ with the highest reputation within his tribe, and men of reputation attract cases from beyond the small group span which they 'represent', as do councillors. In fact, his present local prestige rests almost entirely on his prominence as a _komiti_, for his participation in business enterprises has lagged behind that of many other people. At the same time he has had some reward from this prestige, whereas Nip, with his own business in an equally poor state and after several years' work 'for the government', was recently rejected. He is now dismissed as having been a man 'without talk'.

Official recognition came first in 1966 with an issue of badges from council funds. A new title, _memba_, was widely canvassed. The _komiti_'s status was rationalised as membership of

---

[1] Previous village officials had never been paid; but the _komiti_'s comparison here was with the councillors.

a 'ward committee', although, as Reay (1970:533) points out is the case in Wahgi, komiti are dyadically linked to their common councillor rather than to one another, and the 'committee' as such does not hold meetings or otherwise act as a body. Following this came plans to introduce elections for komiti at the same time as council elections, and much-discussed proposals to provide the elected komiti with incomes. The Dei Council rule for komiti elections was formulated in late 1968,[1] the Mt Hagen Council rule in mid-1970. The Mt Hagen Council's restriction of four komiti per ward was explained to the people as an economic necessity, if wages were to be given to the newly elected.

During my stay komiti elections took place in one Mt Hagen Council tribe. The proposed reduction in numbers (to four)[2] sharpened competition in the electioneering. This particular ward had eleven existing komiti, the plurality being directly related to its composition: a number of small units were scattered over a wide geographical area, each wanting representation. Rivalry thus arose over which would 'win' a komiti this time. If units were left leaderless, who then would supervise government work? Would there be no-one to hold courts? Public speeches held on days preceding this election and on election-day itself stressed the amount of often thankless work which komiti had to do, and constantly mentioned demands made on them to settle disputes.

An ex-councillor pointed out:

> Being a komiti is not a cushy job: you komiti don't just sit down and eat and think of your own business or your house [i.e., your own affairs] - no - you always have to be settling disputes [lit. 'running after courts', kongon kot ile mint pip rok anderemen]. Whether it is a pig or a hen.people steal or if there's a case of adultery or whatever, you have to settle it. I used to be a councillor, and I didn't stay in one place, I just ran after courts and ran after government work, matters to do with work only, and could never take breath.

A young man, who described himself as an 'ordinary chap', that is he was not a councillor or komiti, said:

---

[1] This gave the council as a body power to dismiss komiti. Informal 'elections' seem to have been held in certain areas for some time before this.

[2] Though some people had understood they were to have six komiti, the electorate being composed of members of two tribal groups. There were ten candidates.

> Before we elected councillors and now in the same way we are electing _komiti_, and we should choose from among the old _komiti_. What do new men have to offer? They have one kind of work: to settle disputes, and the men who settle disputes are here. What new work has arisen that we should elect new men? Only one law exists for _komiti_ - to settle disputes.

Here, as in common parlance, Hageners referred to _komiti_ and councillors' handling of disputes as 'hearing courts' (_kot pili_).

A speech given by _komiti_ Karingk after the results of the election were declared, in which he was confirmed in his office, is worth noting:

> You _komiti_ [naming the winners] must think carefully as you take your _komiti_ badges. I, too, must realise that I am someone who has an office [Pidgin _namba_], and must take thought as I put on my badge. Councillor M is like a no. 1 _kiap_, like the DC, and we _komiti_ are no. 2 _kiap_. And you _komiti_ - you must not quarrel with your wives, fight with your brothers, be angry with your fathers, you must take good thought and hear courts [_e pilik kae etek kot pilei_].... If we fight or quarrel we shall lose: if we hear courts badly and anger people, then when the election comes up we shall fall. So think well and always observe this: do your work properly.

Having said that _komiti_ should set a good example in lawful behaviour, he then told the people that they should in the first instance bring their troubles to the _komiti_ they had elected, and only bother councillors over big issues.[1] If the _komiti_ were unable to conclude settlement, then they themselves would refer the case to a councillor. This echoed a remark I heard on another occasion: that _komiti_ are really closer to the ordinary people, they work together with the people, whereas councillors 'work with' the _kiap_.

Reports may be given by _komiti_ to councillors. The _komiti_ will mention cases he has settled and give his own opinion on matters he has been unable to handle satisfactorily. A junior _komiti_ is

---

[1] In 1965-66, when komiti were first officially recognised, people were told by their councillor that it was now the _komiti_'s work to hear all the courts, and only if these 'went wrong' should they bring them to the councillors.

likely to be more scrupulous about this than one who feels himself the equal of his councillor in dispute-settlement. It is a custom between some komiti and some councillors rather than a rule. The reports provide the councillor with background information should the dispute arise again. It is also said to be a check on the activities of komiti. In the words of an ex-councillor: komiti are tied to a councillor like threads through a needle; a councillor is like a man with many wives who judges the merits of each one. A junior komiti making a report may explicitly seek praise for his judicial skill or confirmation of a judgment. The councillor perhaps quizzes him on a compensation arrangement, asking why he let it go at two rather than three items, and so on. It would be unusual, however, for a councillor to interfere with a komiti's decision unless he were approached independently by the disputing parties. The main thing is that for the moment at least the issue has 'died'. Sometimes a komiti informs his councillor when he is on his way to a court, giving the latter an opportunity to offer brief advice on principles to be borne in mind or on the order of compensation payments that would be appropriate.

If a court is not going well, the komiti may call in the councillor, and hope that his judgments will be upheld, that the councillor will say, 'My komiti is like a no.2 kiap and why do you bighead with my komiti?' Komiti regard themselves as usually less hard on people than are councillors, more willing to see an affair settled for a small compensation, and liable to speak in a less trenchant ('hot') manner. But if, for all this, people block the way to agreement, then recourse to the councillor is the only solution.

The election reference to 'hearing courts well' was to the komiti's desire and ability to achieve genuine settlement rather than just gratify his immediate supporters. Indeed, it was said that people judge a komiti by his impartiality, and someone who is seen to help only his own friends or to take advantage of the troubles brought to him,[1] will find that he is not re-elected. And people were told on this occasion to bear in mind the qualities of the men they were about to elect. They should be men who had 'good talk'. This refers to two things. In the first place, a komiti's talk must 'go straight' - he gives due consideration to troubles which are brought to him, shows an understanding of the issues and deliberates on the consequences of the actions he recommends, unlike a child (as it is put) who gabbles insignificantly and utters the first thing that comes into his head. He is responsible for 'his people' and must care

---

[1] Some, like some councillors, are reported to have married women after engineering divorces for them.

for them in the same way as a big-man. Like a councillor, moreover, he is someone who acts as a 'wireless' between the people and the kiap, 'carrying talk' to and fro. In particular, a komiti will have to know how to take cases to a kiap and be able to speak in front of Europeans without shame. For this reason his talk must be strong.[1]

The following reflection on how komiti are chosen reiterates these points. The speaker is an ex-komiti himself.

> We people, we look at the ways of the komiti. Does he settle disputes [lit. 'make courts die'] or straighten courts, does his talk go straight, do we like him [i.e., for these reasons]? A man who can get up in a public ceremonial ground and make speeches when the people are gathered there, and can speak in front of everyone, a man who has no shame before the people or before the kiap, a man who can talk - this is the man we like.

Komiti, like councillors, are thus given a double anchoring. They are seen to have many of the traditional characteristics of big-men. But they are also described as being involved with government work (gavman kongon) - they are gavman rópwu[e] (government helpers) or gavman komiti as distinct from misin pren (mission-friend) and this link with the government is as important for their standing as dispute-settlers as are their big-man qualities. The assumption is that settling disputes will inevitably bring them into contact with kiap and the official courts, so they must have some knowledge of white men's ways.[2] It is also an assumption that one of the tasks of a councillor or komiti is to bring to the people the 'law' of the government, and that the relevance of this should penetrate to the smallest trouble which arises.

---

[1] There has recently been some controversy over the institution of women komiti. Mul and Dei Councils now elect women, one to each ward (not included in figures above), but Mt Hagen councillors have refused to take this step. They argue that women 'have no talk' and cannot possibly deal in matters involving confrontation with the authorities. In the council areas where women are elected, men describe their work as restricted to marshalling women when a workforce is needed, and perhaps to settling minor female squabbles: they do not hear courts as male komiti do. In short, women as a category are regarded as persons whose words rarely carry weight, so that they can act as komiti only in a very limited capacity.

[2] 'Young men can tell the kiap what the people say and tell the people what the kiap says. But the old men don't understand the law of the government' - from the election speeches.

At council meetings _kiap_ give instructions and advice to the councillors who relay this to the _komiti_ and people, and the councillors themselves formulate resolutions and rules. All these may be known as _lo_ ('law'). They also provide occasions on which councillors attempt to sort out their precise relationship with _kiap_. A frequent topic of discussion is their respective roles in hearing courts.

Councillors and _komiti_ both, of course, lack any official magisterial powers. The original _Native Local Government Councils Ordinance_ 1949-60 authorised councils to 'maintain peace, order and good government' in their areas, but did not endow persons with any specifically magisterial duties. In the present _Local Government Ordinance_ 1963, which came into effect in 1965, even this authorisation has been excised, and the main business of councils is rendered as the control, management and administration of the council area. At council meetings the council adviser may bring up the question of 'hearing courts' and point out that councillors technically cannot hold court proceedings, cannot levy fines and cannot act as policemen.

This message runs parallel to (where it is not obscured by) official encouragement of councillors and _komiti_ to act as mediators in 'out-of-court' settlement. Over and again the council minutes record an adviser recommending that councillors should cope with minor troubles themselves, and councillors' own appreciation that _kiap_ are often too busy to be able to deal with every case. One speaker at the _komiti_ elections mentioned above, suggested that a reason why the government had felt it necessary to hold elections was because those who were not hearing courts satisfactorily had to be demoted. The elections were described by ordinary people as a government affair.

Apart from discussions on specific problems, such as divorce rates, bridewealth rules, theft in the town, and the like, questions about courts were raised at 12 of the 44 general meetings held by Mt Hagen Council between March 1967 and October 1970. Basic to all these was a concern as to how disputes should be most effectively handled.[1] Some discussions were held on procedure and included suggestions that there should be a ruling so that councillors could hear courts (in official terms, 'mediate disputes') in relative privacy or that there should be some limit on the number of times a case could be heard. Others centred on sanctions which councillors had at their disposal: one idea was

---

[1] Epstein (1969), who gives a detailed account of the powers and functions of Tolai councillors, notes that Tolai councils 'have repeatedly sought the setting up of [native] courts' (1969:262).

put forward that policemen or Local Court Magistrates should be stationed at each patrol post; another that courts ('mediations') be held in the council chambers or a special court-house; and a resolution was adopted to appoint a number of duty councillors to assist at Local Court hearings.[1] Finally, a frequent question was, given the limits on officials' time, what kind of courts should be taken to the kiap or to the LCM? Several requests were also made by councillors that these magistrates should set aside definite periods during which councillors and komiti could bring them cases to settle.

The constant recommendation of council advisers was that 'major offences' should be dealt with by the sub-district office or LCM or be taken to the police, while 'minor offences' should be settled by councillors and komiti. Individuals differed no doubt in their terminology, but Pidgin records of meetings, as written by the council clerk, show a free use of the term kot. One kiap is recorded as complaining that people should not trouble the sub-district office with pipia ('rubbish') kot over debts, women and pigs; another that liklik ('little') kot could be settled at home. Discussion on the councillors' side was also couched in terms of the kot with which they had to deal. Although kot can mean no more than 'trouble', it is ambiguous in this context. A common interpretation put on discussions of this kind by Hageners is that kiap welcome and support the efforts of councillors and komiti in hearing courts, especially ones which can be concluded easily, and that in doing so the latter are carrying out work for the government.

Settlement at home

Komiti and councillors[2] are likely to conduct preliminary investigations into any case brought to their notice, even if they decide subsequently that it should be turned over to (say) the police. If they can achieve settlement they usually will, so

---

[1] A resolution was made by Dei Council in 1965 to establish a 'council court' comprising two members who would sit in the council house on a set day of the week. Explicit support for this came from the council adviser. By 1970 there were three such councillors ('duty councillors'), whom the present adviser encourages to sort out 'minor' disputes (marriages, debts, pigs); he will back a councillor's decision, he said, where it is a fair one. I heard them referred to as 'siaman [chairman] bilong kot'.

[2] Except where it is clear from the context, I use the terms interchangeably to describe the jobs which either councillor or komiti may do.

that their unofficial jurisdiction includes criminal matters.[1] The number of cases they attempt to handle themselves increases with distance from magisterial centres. Everywhere it is recognised that the gravest offences should be reported to the authorities, according to the dictum of scale of the *kiap*, but the definition of what constitutes such an offence will vary to some extent according to the practicability of laying a report. Other factors include the personalities and ambitions of councillors, political relations between groups, and, in places away from the town, the reputation of locally based officials (such as council adviser). Some grave offences may also be seen chiefly from the point of view of their political repercussions and are judged to be best dealt with at home. Outside interference in such situations might be resented. The degree to which a dispute is treated as a political matter will depend on many factors, including the strategies of local leaders and the perceived power of official agencies.

Similar issues also affect the choices individuals make in whether to seek out the help of a councillor or *komiti*, who themselves sometimes express feelings of responsibility towards keeping people law-abiding. Clans or tribes involved in a conspicuous crime such as homicide profess anxiety lest they acquire a collective reputation for lawlessness. Such a concern, linked closely to a concern for prestige, is echoed in the councillor's or *komiti*'s desire that his people should not be known as trouble-makers. Since this is a personal matter, one finds that individuals differ widely in their expressed attitudes. But it is probably true that on the whole councillors and *komiti* try to deal with most troubles that arise.

They do not, however, interfere in private affairs, that is, investigate matters uninvited. Disputes which are allowed to erupt in public attract general attention, although a *komiti* who has not been directly consulted may choose whether to 'know' about them or not. He may take note, for example, that so-and-so is bleeding from a head wound but wait until he is approached before asking any questions. In brief, *komiti* do not perform police or watchman duties, going around looking for troubles, but wait until troubles are brought to them.

Sometimes a *komiti* refuses to hear cases. The disputants may be too closely related to him, so that he or they prefer someone else to convene the court. This also holds, of course, if he himself becomes a disputant. A complaint may be dismissed as trivial, and women often find themselves turned back for this reason.

---

[1] As Barnett (1967:98) has described for courts held by the then Port Moresby Local Government Council.

Although individual _komiti_ settle small affairs alone, any case which attracts spectators can also attract several _komiti_ or councillors, once a person has approached one such man, without specific invitation. They will be expected to take part in the proceedings. The figures I quoted earlier of the number of cases 'heard' by _komiti_ Nip and Karingk include occasions where other _komiti_ were present. While usually an individual will go first to the _komiti_ closest to him (unless he is too close), he often has the chance to take his grievance to several men. He may select a _komiti_ for his reputation or for his knowledge of previous disputes between the same people. The existence of such a choice is backed to some extent by the ideology that these persons, as a category, all do a similar job and should carry it out with as much impartiality as possible. It is true that _komiti_ are also looked to for support. Support is given most ostensibly in a readiness to listen to complaints (their accessibility) and in the trouble to which _komiti_ sometimes have to go to arrange a meeting between the relevant parties. On occasion they may act as defence counsel, although this does not bar them (as Hageners see it) from taking an impartial view later in the proceedings.

Impartiality is part of the image which councillors and _komiti_ project of themselves in the context of dispute-settlement. In fact, local leaders may be acting in their own interests, or in the interests of groups or categories of people, or they may try to seek the best compromise between competing interests. Often people go to them with appeals to represent them in a court confrontation. For _komiti_ have to manipulate two roles: the bigman who is a champion and the law-man who is an arbiter.[1] But by comparison with the criticism which people voice about councillors becoming too distracted by other duties to attend properly to disputes at home, complaints are not often made in the open about this. Individuals have different reputations for fairness (and these, of course, vary according to one's point of view). But councillors and _komiti_ are more likely to be criticised on the grounds of settling a case 'badly', because they are weak and ineffective, or for being poor speech-makers, than they are simply on grounds of corruption.[2] As in the conduct of public affairs in general, it is known that men placed into the position of

---

[1] Hide (1971:55-6) illustrates the ways in which members of land demarcation committees in Chimbu may act as representatives of claimants or as mediators between claimants. He suggests that ambiguity lies within the role of 'committee member' itself.

[2] As, for example, seems to be a point in criticisms Sinasina make of their councillors (Hatanaka 1972:73).

hearing disputes are likely to be juggling various strategies, and must balance the different requirements made of their roles.

The attribute of impartiality is stressed more by councillors and komiti than by ordinary people. At one tribal meeting in 1965 (Mt Hagen Council area), when proposals for the new badges were discussed, the then councillor of the tribe tried to impress on the assembly that they should not think of komiti as members of this or that subclan but as locally based persons to whom all kinds of people could bring their troubles. When allied clans from different tribes are neighbours it is common for the komiti or councillor of one to take an interest in the affairs of the other. At a court I attended in 1964, a councillor of tribe M welcomed a speech from a colleague of tribe N by saying:

> He has come to live with the M, and M and N hold courts together. The kiap has marked all the councillors as above everyone else, to hear courts as a body.

In effect he was saying that they should ignore tribal differences in the interests of a common job.[1] And people often ask how settlement can be reached if councillors and komiti are unable to stand apart from the disputants. When clans meet in confrontation, councillors on opposing sides may publicly reassure one another that they have no intention of just 'helping' their own group. Proclaimed one councillor in 1970:

> Do you over there think that I just want to help so-and-so? I hear courts, and help the men of my own clan, and I fail to help the courts of other clans, is this how I act, then? But if I did do this, you would say I was a bad councillor and go off and gossip about me .... I am a big-man and can hear the talk of A and the talk of B, and can straighten both talks.

Claims to impartiality can be used rhetorically and are certainly not always taken at face value by the audience. They may, indeed, be brought in to draw attention away from bias. Thus women often find themselves at a disadvantage in unofficial courts, where a councillor may be so afraid he will be accused of 'helping' them that he hardly gives their case a fair hearing. Nevertheless, these claims are part of the ideology of court hearings.

---

[1] M and N were opponents in this dispute; the councillor was appealing to common ground (their councillorship and neighbourhood ties) to provide a basis on which agreement could be built.

The public maintenance of avowed impartiality broke down at one stage in the poison trials mentioned in Chapter 2. The questioning of the woman[1] followed a few days after a critical confrontation between members of tribes X and W. During this the councillors present were upbraided for allowing the talk to get out of hand, and thereby defeating the whole purpose of the meeting, because they had turned it from a judicial inquiry into a political debate.

Case 5: the poison confrontation. It had taken a long time for members of tribe X to persuade the W to attend any meeting at all. Most active here was the X councillor, Malt, and councillors and *komiti* were the most prominent speakers when eventually they assembled near the sub-district office on the afternoon of a market Saturday. The crowd of spectators they attracted swelled to over 500. The atmosphere was tense: X, first covertly and then openly, accused W of attempting to poison them. It was a political contest, at which only the most important men spoke. For this reason it is interesting to note what a large proportion of the men were or had been village officials of some kind.[2]

The intention had certainly been to hold a court hearing. Unfortunately the W had failed to bring along with them the young wife, Neng, so that the cross-questioning of Neng and her sister Kurup had to be postponed. It was apparent that without her there could be no conclusion to the debate. But talk raged for four hours. The X could not hope to reassemble everyone again (indeed, the later questioning of the two girls (Case 2) was a much smaller affair), and this was the time to display to the W their anger at having been targets for poison; the W revealed their own anger at this attack.

It was well known that the Administration was not really interested in poison and was unlikely to treat the suspicions seriously. Nevertheless, this anger had to be contained. The very fact that the sub-district office was chosen as a venue suggests that the

---

[1] See Case 2, p.32ff.

[2] Of the 29 speakers (apart from persons who made interjections), 14 were councillors (8) or *komiti* (6), including an ex-president of Mt Hagen Council. A further 5 had served a term as councillor or been a *luluai*, *tultul* or *bosboi*. Another speaker was a current government interpreter. The total of officials or ex-officials was thus 20. Of the remainder, at least 7 were recognised big-men; one of the non-big-men was required to speak because of his special relations with the Z girls who were involved as witnesses.

big-men hoped there would be an ultimate curb on violence, and this may have been one reason why they were so free with their tongues. Feelings about the past were given vent. Former contests were referred to and the names of important dead men on each side were recited. At the same time other old facts about their relationship were also recalled: although W and X were enemies, in the distant past there had been no suspicion of poison between them. Speech after speech referred to the fact that the days of fighting were long since over, and it would be a regression to return to them. So the present confrontation was an anomaly: a 'new' thing, poison between the two tribes, was alleged to have occurred but, as speech-makers reminded people, they were also 'new men' who were standing here now, who held law in their hands, who ran businesses, and who, unlike their fathers, did not fight with weapons.[1]

The meeting degenerated into verbal brawling at more than one point. The first brought men to their feet, and they remained standing until the end. Almost everyone momentarily joined in the accusations and counter-accusations that were brazenly shouted out ('You are the owner of the poison!'), before some began trying to calm down others. Councillors and komiti, other than the main disputants, were prominent in trying to restore order. While the whole occasion bred considerable excitement, and no-one was surprised at the turn of events, people knew it would be too dangerous to let themselves get carried away. Much of the speech-making included comments on how far short of a proper court the discussion was falling.

One point of criticism was bandied between the two sides: X accused W of not bringing with them the key witness, Neng. They had brought 'their own woman', Kurup, as had been arranged, but how could anything be discussed without Neng? It was the W's duty to go and get her, and thereby show both their responsibility for her and their willingness to thrash out the problem. Failure to bring her simply pointed to guilt. Among the various circumstantial excuses which W made of why it had been impossible to bring her, they protested that if they had brought the girl themselves they would only have been accused of influencing what she said, and that on the contrary they wanted to hold a fair examination. Patently it was up to X to fetch her. Commonsense suggestions, such as that a pair of men, one from X and one from W hire a car and find the witness, were made into the late afternoon, with everyone knowing that nothing would happen. Points of procedure were being used here rhetorically as weapons of attack, in the way that appeals to values often are.

---

[1] At the time when this was spoken (1970), there had been no major outbreaks of fighting concerning these groups for many years.

Another point of criticism, levelled both by village officials and other big-men, was that some of the councillors were acting irresponsibly in encouraging 'angry talk' (ik m^e^ra) instead of 'quiet talk' (ik raka raka). One young rising big-man named two of the protagonists, councillor Malt of X and Nggomb of W, an ex-tultul who was among the chief suspects in X's eyes.

> They shout at one another, and why do they? Has a pig gone into one of their gardens, are they quarrelling over the garden or sweet potato plants [i.e., that have been damaged]? Malt, you are a councillor; Nggomb, before you were a tultul. You are men who have heard law. And when a pig is killed or something is stolen, you question people and find out, and in the same way let's ask and we can find out about this matter. Why do you talk angrily for no reason? Let's investigate it properly [lit. 'look well'] and the pair [the two sisters] can come and talk and then we shall see. Where did they find the poison? We can ask the two of them, that is all right. But you quarrel and talk too much, and we'll stop this. When you hear courts you ask, what men killed the pig? Do you want to arrange compensation? You hear courts quietly, easily, I know this. But now W gets up and talks, and X gets up and talks, you talk against each other, and I feel your words do not go straight. Where is the witness? Woman, who slept with you? Who chased the pig? This is what is asked in courts, quietly and without fuss, and so we see the root of the court.[1] But now you W and you X are just quarrelling and where now is the root of the talk?

On several occasions I have heard a contrast drawn between the kind of 'talk' appropriate for courts and that which characterises other public meetings. Oratory is highly developed in Hagen, and it is the big-man in particular who is distinguished by his skills at public speaking. Elaborate speeches accompany ceremonial exchange displays, in which the donors of a gift vaunt their own munificence and taunt recipients. The words, full of political innuendo, become highly charged. This type of oratory is called 'war (or arrow) talk'. More than one person during the poison confrontation said that all the speeches belonged to the realm of

---

[1] Kot raka raka weng ndok nik mondei ik pukli kandep køneimin. Pukli or pukl ('root') here refers to the reason for the trouble, whose revelation brings some hope of solution (see Chapter 2).

ceremonial exchange and that the rhetoric used was the kind their fathers and grandfathers engaged in when they thought of fighting. Characteristic of this style [1] is the compressed use of allusions and metaphors which render many statements 'double talk' (ik ek). The intention is to convey different meanings to different persons who might be in the audience, perhaps to speak offensively without giving concrete grounds for accusation on this score. Such speech-making is felt to be directly opposed to the kind of talk suitable for a judicial inquiry - it confuses issues, piles on layers of meaning, and deliberately fosters multiple interpretations, rather than coming to the heart of a conflict; above all, it is the language of confrontation rather than compromise. Hageners put the contrast succinctly: between mbo ik (in this context 'traditional oratory') and kotnga ik ('talk to do with courts').

Courts, then, should engender particular attitudes: a degree of impartiality in councillors and komiti, and willingness on the part of disputants to talk out the issues in the interest of a solution. There are also certain procedural notions about the evaluation of evidence and use of witnesses. It is desirable that all the relevant[2] disputants should be present. When, at the poison confrontation, men of tribe Z said they had questioned the girls and this had revealed nothing, X men pointed out that that could not be more than a 'half court', the talk of just one side, since they themselves had not been present on the occasion. Insofar as such points are adhered to, we may speak of these proceedings having formality. There is, however, little physical formality in their conduct.

Conducting a case

Hearings are located according to convenience - in a private courtyard, on a ceremonial ground, or wherever the assembly is inclined. Specific rules govern neither this nor seating arrangements. People cluster casually, usually in some kind of circle, with each speaker in turn becoming the focus of attention. Knots of men may break away, presenting their backs to the speakers to whom they are still listening, to light fires or engage in other minor activities. There is no rule about where councillors or komiti[3] should sit, or where the disputants should be in relation

---

[1] For examples see A.J. Strathern (1971:appendix 7).

[2] Though relevance is open to definition - see A.M. Strathern (1972:219ff.) for an example of a divorce court held in the absence of the husband.

[3] Again, I subsequently refer to only one or other but either councillors or komiti may be involved.

to them. The audience is free to come and go. Variations exist according to the type of hearing, but komiti usually begin by taking a chairman's role, inviting the different parties to speak in turn[1] and keeping order while they do so. They then cross-examine as seems appropriate, call witnesses, and begin in their speeches to move towards suggestions of how the matter can be solved. These suggestions will include references to the placement of culpability. Culpability is shared when it is recommended that more than one party find a compensation item. There is no formal charge or declaration that so-and-so is guilty separate from the decision of a penalty. Komiti may, however, assume a very clear initiative in both recommending what would be appropriate damages and demanding that specific items be paid in recognition of the 'crime'.

Three current terms, by origin Pidgin but absorbed into Melpa, refer to categories of compensation payments: baim ofis, baim kot, and baim lo ('to buy office ... court ... law'). These are not direct translations of Melpa categories, for which Pidgin phrases can also be given, for example, sek han ('shake hands') for ki titimbil, or baim het bilong man ('to pay for a man's head'), a type of war indemnity (wu^{e} peng). Rather they can be used generally to refer to any compensation-settlement having been agreed upon through a court, whether heard by a kiap, LCM, councillor or komiti.[2] Hageners use all three terms for payments which are decided on in the courts of formal settlement.

The terms have an official resonance about them. Baim kot (which is correct Local Court language for court fine) refers not only to unofficial court proceedings conducted by councillors but to the Local Court and the fines it imposes, in the same way as the term it is now superseding, baim ofis,[3] referred to the subdistrict office and the fines which kiap used to demand. Baim lo is also a relatively new term[4] and directly refers to the fact

---

[1] First the accuser and then the accused, if this structure is appropriate; but proceedings really start from when the first complaint is lodged, and if the facts are patent to everyone, the defendant may be called on to speak straight away.

[2] Ceremonial exchanges focused upon war or ally payments would not now be described in this way, although in the past the decision to make such payments may have followed a 'dispute-settling' procedure.

[3] One ex-luluai said that he was told by a kiap to call compensations decided on by him (the luluai) baim ofis.

[4] I hardly heard it during my stay in 1964-65.

that dispute-settling agencies are concerned with keeping the law. In the same way as big-men 'give talk', modern councillors and komiti 'give lo' (lo ngui) when agreement is finally reached. They may lecture the wrong-doer on the folly of his actions, or tell the plaintiff that even though he is now receiving compensation money, were he to do the same thing then he, too, would have to pay damages.

Some people assert that the three terms have different meanings. One may say that baim kot is just another term for baim ofis and corresponds to the Melpa kumøp, which in property offences refers to restitution, whereas baim lo is the extra item given on top. Another may say that baim lo is the restitution payment and baim kot is that which is paid in addition when the affair is taken to the Local Court (i.e., a court fine); another that baim lo is a new term for baim ofis and both refer to an additional payment. Basic to all these are attempts to construct a dichotomy in the elements of compensation. This follows their own category distinctions between 'restitution' and 'reconciliation'. It is supported by those judgments in the Local Court, few as they are, which direct both restitution and penalty. It is interesting that Hageners find it easy to equate these with their own categories, because at first sight reconciliation seems far removed from penalty.

When a case is taken to the Local Court, the aggrieved party may say, 'If he is not going to make a payment to me, then he can go to jail'. This is not simply a sanction ('You will go to jail if you do not pay me') but recognises an equivalence between the two alternatives open to the defendant, which is based on Hageners' own ideas about punishment. In addition to the distinction between restitution and reconciliation items, compensation ought, it is felt and was felt traditionally, to both satisfy the complainant and (indicated in the same or an additional item) punish the offender. The phrases baim kot or baim lo are often used to express the idea that apart from injury or damage to another person, a definite wrong has been committed. This is fully upheld by what Hageners see of the workings of the official courts, which give weight to punishment. In the past, punishment existed both through provision of compensation to the plaintiff and through other means (e.g., retaliation), and in a sense the official courts provide just another avenue. Someone unable to gain monetary compensation will nevertheless express personal satisfaction if his complaints result in the offender having to go to jail or pay a large court fine.

But there is also a more direct equation between paying for 'breaking the law of the government' (which should bring punishment) and the traditional custom of adding a reconciliation item to a restitution payment. For payments given in token of the desire for 'reconciliation' necessarily indicate that an injury has been done to social relations. In the case of unilateral guilt, balance is restored by a penalty imposed on the wrong-doer. The notion of paying for such a wrong is in this sense an element contained within 'reconciliation' gifts. To be made to hand over payments for breaking the law also fits into Hagen concepts that bigger compensations should be paid when the trial has been a long and difficult one because the wrong-doer has refused to admit his guilt.

There are no rigid rules, however, about the way in which payments under different rubrics should be made, and they occur in various permutations. I give a brief example of one. A pig was stolen from inside the enclosure of a komiti belonging to a clan allied to the thief's own. A komiti from the thief's clan ordered that he make in effect three payments: a pig to replace the stolen animal (restitution, in Melpa kumøp), but one that should be larger than the original 'because you have broken the law of the government', an element referred to by the Melpa yoka ('an additional reconciliation item'), and finally $20 'because you have broken the fence' (pakla mbruk ndok) between the two clans. Here both the yoka and the pakla items were to restore the friendly relations the thief had upset, the latter specifically because the thief had also trespassed into the area of another group, the former in recognition of his general fault in the matter.[1]

I here anticipate some of my later argument about relations between the official and unofficial courts but have done so to make explicable the kind of emphasis which councillors and komiti place on making these payments. In suggesting that extra items, or a single item especially large, should be given in addition to an initial payment, some stress the importance of reconciliation in preventing future troubles, others that such impositions punish the offender. These principles, then, are both aspects of 'law and order', and by using the rubrics baim kot or baim lo, they remind people that, in maintaining law and order, councillors and komiti are agents of the government.

Two cases told to me by Kar, a young and rather inexperienced komiti, illustrate this, and also introduce some further points.

Case 6: the family fight. A father and son quarrelled over the upkeep of a coffee garden, and their wives became caught up in the fighting. The son's wife, with wounds of her own, came running to the komiti to say that her husband's head was broken open. The komiti was horrified at the extent of the man's wounds,

---

[1] See A.M. Strathern (1972:229-31) for a discussion of compensation terms. Those quoted here follow Central Melpa usage.

and thought of sending him to the police station, but it was at night[1] and there were no means of getting there. The following day he asked the injured man if he would like the matter taken to the councillor or whether he himself (the komiti) should conclude it, and the young man said it was all right for the komiti to do so. The issues were discussed. It came out that the father had at one point been only just restrained by someone else from using a knife. This person spoke out as a witnes (witness). The father was told that for wounding his child he had done wrong (lit. 'it was not just', kapokla) and broken the law. And for threatening him with the knife he had also broken gavman lo ('government law'), for the government has made rules against people using weapons. So Kar decided that the father should pay two items, $10 and a pig, which were handed over to the son. The komiti asked the son if he was satisfied or if he wanted to go to the councillor, and the son said that his 'heart was now good'. The money was for threatening with the knife, the pig for the wounds, and both came under a traditional rubric ('payment for spilt blood'). Kar spoke to the father: 'You know the law, and if I were to take you to the kiap you would have to make a huge payment. But I am sorry for you, and did not call in the police. I would make you pay an extra item for baim lo, but you have already given enough'. The son kept the pig, but he distributed the money. He gave $2 to komiti Kar, $4 to various people who had been present during the court, $2 to those who had spoken as witnesses, and kept the remainder himself. The payment to the komiti was referred to as money to buy tobacco, a small token for his hard work in conducting the court.

Komiti and councillors differ in their techniques and approaches to solving problems. Some have reputations for hard talk, some for leniency, some for wit and sarcasm. They may try to shame people into heeding their advice, or use blatant threats. The soft-heartedness of this particular komiti comes out again in Case 7.

Case 7: the lad who killed his uncle's pig. A pig was missing, and the owner (and others) suspected two youths of the locality, one of whom was his own brother's son. There was no direct evidence, but the nephew's father and the wife of the other young man both spoke as witnesses to the fact that the pair had not been home the previous night. The young men would reveal nothing

---

[1] While at home, a komiti can be approached at any time of day or night but may grumble if people are unreasonable. Kar pointed out, 'A kiap doesn't work at night and hear courts. It is time to sleep and I want to go to sleep - come back in the morning'.

until the komiti drew them aside and asked them in secret; they admitted to having killed and eaten a pig, making the conventional excuse that they did not know whose it was. They agreed with the komiti's suggestion that each provide an animal - only one had been killed, on the initiative of the other young man, but the nephew had to provide a pig as well because instead of looking after his father's brother's animal, he had helped the thief. In addition they would pay $5 each for baim lo. The pigs were to make the uncle's heart feel good, while the money symbolised the fact that they were being punished for a crime. Komiti Kar then went back to the assembled court but was afraid that, if too direct a statement were made of the youths' guilt, the uncle would become incensed. He covered up for them (a device that would be understood by his hearers) by saying he did not know if they really had killed the pig or not, but he had told them to provide two pigs in compensation, and was the owner satisfied? The komiti, according to his own account, took the $10 to the then LCM.[1] One of the pigs was killed by the owner and everyone, including the komiti, who had taken part in the court shared in its consumption. It was the komiti's own touch to encourage the two youths to remain and eat with them. He said that if there was to be no trouble later, then they must all sit down and 'shake hands' and eat together.

This, in fact, is contrary to usual procedure, where the person who yields compensation is expected to feel too badly about it to stay and consume his own animal. Here, one of the thieves had taken his own father's brother's pig and this man was extremely angry; it was desirous that evidence should be given of their reconciliation. Sometimes, indeed, culprits may share in the meal of the pig they have provided in compensation for precisely the opposite reason: komiti Karingk described how, when he was dealing with an inveterate pig thief, he would force the thief to eat part of the compensation pig 'to make him feel', that is as a punishment.

> Let the thief come and see how his pig is being butchered, what a lot of fat it has [i.e., what a good size it would have grown to], and eat some of it, so that he will remember later when his clansmen collect together their pigs for display in ceremonial exchange that he, too, could have contributed a magnificent beast. However angry this may make the thief at the time, he will think twice before stealing again, and in the end settle down to a quiet life.

---

[1] Neither the LCM nor kiap accept money brought to them, but this komiti clearly presented himself as behaving with exemplary rectitude, for which he says he gained the LCM's praise.

In Case 7 *komiti* Kar, as was traditional custom, shared in the compensation pig.[1] In Case 6 he received part of the payment; as was also traditional, the amount was not dictated by the *komiti* but given out of the sum awarded to the plaintiff. The plaintiff may choose to give nothing at all. If he does make a small present this is to show his gratitude to those who went to the trouble of convening and conducting the court; thus, in addition to the *komiti*, others present, including witnesses, may receive a small item or share of meat. Although the amounts are generally insignificant ($1 or $2, enough to buy a packet of cigarettes, Hageners say), and are intended to compensate the *komiti* for work he had not been able to do in his gardens while he was hearing the court, *komiti* themselves may compare it to the income which councillors receive. It is certainly true that since cases are brought to them more regularly than they would have been to big-men in the past, these office-holders do more regularly receive such gifts. These are usually given, however, only after disputes of some magnitude. Their chief importance lies in the recognition of the *komiti*'s status. Occasionally one hears tales of an extortionist *komiti* or councillor,[2] often a product of the particular viewpoint of persons associated with the case. There is no general questioning by Hageners of the theoretical right of *komiti* and councillors to share in part of the compensation item, along with others. It is regarded as part of the *baim kot* or *baim lo* procedure.

Komiti's idiosyncratic views towards who should participate in the compensation pig may make one man appear anxious to promote reconciliation, another eager to inflict punishment. However, idiosyncracies cannot be given too free a rein. Councillors and *komiti* are seen as persons who conduct courts according to certain generally understood precepts, and the man who strikes out on his own, thinks up devices in his head, and gets carried away by the court situation to impose bizarre penalties, is quickly criticised. 'A *komiti* must give good law, and act to satisfy the feelings of the disputants', one old ex-*tultul* remarked. By this he meant that village officials should follow the recommendations of the *kiap* and also try to meet the needs of local people. Councillors and *komiti* who arbitrarily take things into their own hands are not doing a proper (*kapckla*) job. He was particularly thinking of the way some *komiti* deliberately lie or act partially to help those they favour, or otherwise gain

---

[1] Hatanaka (1972:114) notes a similar convention in Sinasina unofficial courts.

[2] More frequently from Europeans than from Hageners, see Chapter 4.

from a court, or get angry during the dispute and impose too heavy a compensation.

One of the procedures which is probably more formalised now than in the past is that of calling upon witnesses. The Pidgin term (witnes) is used regularly. In the past, peaceful settlement could not be negotiated successfully in the absence of verifiable evidence, but disputants might take various forms of retaliation on the strength of personal suspicions. There is possibly more effort today to seek out people who can provide information. The onus is on the plaintiff to assemble evidence and find witnesses. They are most crucial in cases of theft; many thefts reported to councillors or komiti have to be dropped for lack of witnesses.

A witness must be someone who sees an incident with his eye, does not just hear about it by ear,[1] and preferably be only distantly related to the disputants. Someone may excuse himself from giving evidence because of his intimacy with the defendant. It is also preferable for the testimony of several persons to be heard, unless the words of a single witness lead to further proof. Witnesses are only called in when an accused person denies the charge. He is given his chance to speak first.

What witnesses have to say is generally accepted in good faith although their remarks, like those of the principals, are scrutinised for proof of validity. Sometimes sworn evidence is given, but it is usually the defendant rather than a witness who is asked to swear. Oaths may be taken on traditional objects (the divination-substance mi) or their modern equivalents, such as a coin showing the head of a monarch. Where one of the parties is Christian, or has Christian relatives, beads, crucifixes or religious books may be used. As was the case in the past, the oath establishes overall guilt or innocence rather than the veracity of a single item of information.

The notion of witnes is modelled upon what is known of official courts. There are modifications. The Hagen witness at a councillor's court is usually seen as being on the side of the plaintiff (although the defendant may sometimes be asked if anyone can verify his or her statements). In this sense, the witness may be spoken of as 'courting' the defendant. Komiti Kar referred in this way to the witnesses who appeared in Cases 6 and 7. In Case 6 the chief witness, a married woman from the same settlement as the family, is supposed to have said: 'I am a witness and I

---

[1] The Melpa phrase for a witness is simply 'a man who says what he has seen'.

want to court you' (nim kot indimb, lit. 'I shall put a court on you'); while in Case 7 the komiti told the youths that for one of them it was his own father, for the other his own wife, who were speaking out their suspicions and hence acting as witnesses against them: 'A, your father courts you; B, your wife courts you'. Here the very proximity of relationship lent weight to the evidence. This reveals a common Hagen expectation: a man ordinarily counts on the support of his close kin to keep silent, if not openly to campaign on his behalf. But if these kin reveal things about him, and act as witnesses against him, their lack of support is a clear indication of his guilt. It is assumed that such persons would not speak lightly, and they are taking on themselves the responsibility of exposing him.

Referring cases

A settlement by a komiti normally concludes with a transfer of goods. But not all cases are settled. Disputants often then take the initiative and approach an outside agency. Komiti and councillors themselves go to a kiap or LCM.

It is not possible to indicate all the circumstances under which disputes are taken to Administration agencies. An affair that dissolves into an impasse, or is argued into one, is typical. Also typical are situations where an accused person refuses absolutely to submit to the recommendations of an unofficial court. Councillors then appeal to the kiap or the police, or say they will do so in an effort to persuade the disputants to accept their verdicts. They suggest that these persons are likely to be much more severe than the councillors are themselves, so it is in everyone's interests to have the affair settled at home. Komiti and councillors frequently state that they are supported by the kiap, police or LCM.[1] Someone who does not heed their recommendations compounds his wrongs by acting as a bikhet and lays himself open to threats from the komiti that they will raise the amount of compensation he has to pay, or else that they will jail him (i.e., take him to an official court, where if his wrongs are proved he may have to go to jail). Going to jail in such circumstances is

---

[1] This is partly a matter of dogma. Given their lack of official standing, support for councillors and komiti cannot be automatic. But it seems that instances of imputed support are remembered, whereas instances to the contrary are dismissed as insignificant. It is interesting also to note that compensations paid through the councillors' courts are often higher than fines imposed by the Local Court, especially when pigs are involved; the imputation of severity to the official court is an aspect of Hageners' hierarchical thinking which I comment on later.

looked upon as an equivalent of the extra item a man pays for 'breaking the law' (see above); only occasionally would he also have to make private payments when he comes out of jail. And in the eyes of some councillors and komiti an element of the law-breaking is failure to co-operate in the unofficial court hearing.

The komiti who can make someone yield and pay compensation where others have failed, shows 'strength'. This may be referred to quite openly, so that a komiti or councillor takes up a difficult case because of its challenge to his skill. If the person in the wrong refuses to come to a settlement[1] and the komiti takes him to the police or whoever, it is further evidence of the komiti's strength if these authorities support him, either ordering the man to follow the komiti's own recommendation or else meting out their particular punishment. The komiti may speak of himself as 'winning'.

The contest of strength is played out with police, kiap and the LCM as allies. Not only komiti and councillors test their strength in this way: an ordinary person may choose to bypass the local officials and take his complaints straight to the police station ('I shall jail you!'). Such action is likely to be regarded by the other party as a direct challenge. (And a councillor may take it as a challenge to his own authority as well.)[2] When faced with such aggressive behaviour, a person who professes to have been willing to meet the other's complaints with a small compensation will become aggressive in turn: 'Let us see if he is strong enough to speak to the kiap - if they send out a policeman to fetch me, all right, they can jail me. I am not afraid of jail. But I am going to be strong too, I shall pay him nothing'. People often say in such situations, 'Well, we'll see what the kiap/policeman/LCM says, and if they decide to jail me, they can'. In other words, although the plaintiff may regard the jail sentence as a sign that the authorities are acting in his favour, the defendant regards it as an inevitable repercussion which emanates from outside and cannot therefore be regarded as victory for his opponent. He submits to the authorities, not to the other man's strength. His refusal to come to terms with the opponent, and suffering jail instead, indicates his own strength.

---

[1] And it may be that he is not unwilling to make a small payment but baulks at the large amount which the komiti has suggested 'to teach him not do it again and because he broke the law'.

[2] Beattie (1971:224) describes an African usage of a similar situation: a Nyoro chief adjudicating 'out of court' threatened a recalcitrant offender with formal proceedings if he did not heed the unofficial judgment.

It is not uncommon, then, for disputes to be taken to the official authorities in some spirit of aggressiveness. This may stem from a state of impasse which arguments have reached, or from councillors' frustrations in trying to negotiate a settlement, or it may be something of an hostile act by one of the litigants. Significantly, the action of taking such cases to the authorities is seen as a move to contain this very aggression. It may express hostility but the course of action is non-violent.

The authorities are often seen as appropriate agents to turn to when feelings are on the verge of erupting into violence.[1] This fits in with the Administration's injunction that major issues, such as fighting, wounding and so on, should be reported to the police straight away. Arson also falls into this category, as do other forms of large-scale malicious damage. The final case[2] which I describe is one of malicious damage, in which a decision to take the matter to the police and kiap was made without any attempt at local settlement. The councillor, Malt[3], who took the initiative, is a youngish and forward-looking man, whose one-time experience with the army has made him familiar with official procedure of all kinds. He has a more accurate picture of the workings of the Local Court, for example, than most members of his tribe. The son of a now-deceased big-man, he conducts 'out-of-court' settlements much in the manner of other councillors and komiti, although he does not hesitate to use his wide grasp of Pidgin judicial vocabulary, to the occasional confusion of his co-tribesmen. The case is interesting in that it shows among other things the kinds of expectations that a man of this kind may have of the official judiciary.

Case 8: the case of Timb's house. An area of land lying between settlements occupied by members of tribes X and K had recently come under dispute. For the time being it was agreed in an unofficial court that no further dwelling houses should be built or gardens made there but that men of both tribes would use the land as common pig pasture. Timb, from X, decided to renovate an old pig-house[4] which had fallen into disrepair. This lay within the pasture under dispute. One morning his family arrived at the house

---

1 Not that appeal is made to them in every such case. In areas away from the town especially, people may feel they can cope with a broader spectrum of issues themselves.

2 I disguise certain details here (but not the order of events or attitudes expressed by various participants).

3 The same councillor mentioned in Cases 2 and 5.

4 Of the kind used mainly for stalling pigs, though it might be slept in from time to time.

to find that it had been systematically destroyed: thatch pulled off, walls hacked down, and the building ropes cut through. Trees nearby had been slashed. Timb gathered up some of the severed ropes as evidence. He learnt from his X neighbours that a party of K men had been seen there during the night. These came from families which had been most closely involved in the previous disputes.

Timb made his way as quickly as possible to councillor Malt. Like Timb, Malt interpreted the attack on the house, and in particular the slashing of the trees,[1] as a threat from these men that unless Timb removed his house they would attack him personally, perhaps kill him. Malt took a serious view of the matter. 'They are wild, lawless men', he said, 'Men who do not listen to the people'. He chose to deal with the incident as a threat to peace, and said he was worried in case his people of tribe X took the matter into their hands and delivered a counter-attack. He gave strict orders, and these were heeded, that no-one from X was even to approach the ruined house. If they saw the extent of damage their anger would make them lose self-control. This also safeguarded the evidence, because then the men of K would not be able to accuse X of having rigged the affair.

He left for the sub-district office in Mt Hagen town, where he was given a letter by a kiap to take to the police station. He waited at the station until nightfall, but no vehicles were available. Some of the X men had meanwhile assembled to discuss their fears that a fight would break out. Many openly expressed the hope that the K would have to endure a long jail sentence. 'They humbug with us and can suffer for it.' Malt, disappointed that he had not been able to bring in policemen at once, went early next day to the police station and accompanied a party of police to the K settlements. The K men took a long time to gather together, although they did not hide their part in the affair, expressing defiance over the prospect of jail. They were taken to the police station, questioned but not charged, and then released. According to Malt, the police said that the root of the trouble was land, not the house - if they arrested the K for having attacked the house, the land issue would only come up in court and this was something for DDA. Malt was angry and disappointed. He checked with the LCM, who said it was a police matter and he could not hear any details first.

On the third day Malt, accompanied by others of X, went into town again. He saw another kiap. The kiap said that if the K had a grievance over the land, then they should have come themselves

[1] Cf. Case 3, pp.38-40.

to the sub-district office and arrangements could have been made for investigation by a land demarcation committee. As it was, he confirmed Malt's view that they had done wrong by taking the law into their own hands and destroying the house, and that the police could prosecute on this score. Malt said that they could let the issue of the land lie; he wanted to settle the attack on the house. He went again to the police, who at once agreed to rearrest the K as soon as a car could be found. While the X were waiting for this vehicle, news came to them that the K councillor was willing to talk the matter over at home. A deputation from K arrived and said that they should forget about the town and go and discuss the issues privately. The words were not heeded, the offer being dismissed as <u>tok gris</u> (Pidgin for 'a persuasive trick'). X probably felt they would have been on weaker ground, since then the act of destruction would have been set into the context of encroachment into the disputed area. They preferred to try to prosecute the K in terms of damage to the house. Eventually the K men were rearrested and charged after questioning, and kept in cells overnight.

The case was brought before the LCM the next morning. At the police station both K and X men had been questioned about the incident; but although X were present in court, statements were, of course, only required from the accused K. All the men pleaded guilty and were convicted for having maliciously destroyed some-one else's property. Because of extenuating circumstances the magistrate imposed fairly light fines, but also awarded damages to Timb.

The case shows clearly how the two sides jockeyed for the most advantageous position in which to have the dispute settled (X knew they could count on officially placing a charge for malicious damage, if the issues were kept to the house;[1] K that they could bring up the whole land matter and better justify their actions if a court were held at home), and how one side attempted to use the official judiciary and its penalties to take revenge for the wrong inflicted upon them. The point here, however, is not that revenge-feelings were roused but that, given their existence, they were deflected into non-violent channels. Attitudes which Malt and others of X expressed were significant in this context.

---

[1] I have simplified many of the issues involved. In fact, Malt was later criticised by one of his <u>komiti</u> for not making the X's 'legitimate' claims to the land clear to the authorities, and at one blow getting K convicted of assault and thrown off the land for good.

Malt made no attempt to minimise the anger which X men would have felt at K's act of aggression (as they saw it). Had he tried to drive it underground and ride over the whole affair, things might have developed into an inflammatory impasse. He therefore voiced these feelings but suggested that the proper course of action would be to impose Administration penalties. It was his expressed opinion that if they had tried to settle it at home, it would undoubtedly have led to a fight. The X had no desire to fight[1] and agreed. They were disappointed that the police did not come sooner and that the K got away with fines (rather than having to go to jail). The LCM did, however, reprimand the K for their lawlessness and for taking the matter into their own hands, and the X were openly pleased at this. One may surmise from their attitudes that this was not only because the K had been given a dressing-down but because their respective positions had been recognised. They, the X, could have chosen to ignore the law and retaliate themselves; but since they decided on a different course they looked to the government for approval. Various X said they were relieved the penalties had not been too harsh, because this might just have made the K bitter and desire revenge themselves. But Malt remained a little apprehensive over the light penalty since, in spite of the damages, he was afraid that Timb and his close associates might still start a fight.

This was the clue to his worries throughout the four days: that there was a limit to the extent to which he, as councillor, could restrain his own people. His concern seemed overdone to some of the authorities. He had a quite lengthy conversation with one of them[2] on this point. 'What would happen if a fight came up', asked Malt, 'what would happen to my reputation?' The official with whom he was talking took a kindly view: 'That's all right, it is nothing to do with you. Your reputation won't be harmed. Everyone knows you. If the others want to fight, it is their affair if they are jailed!' 'But', protested Malt, 'I have a hard time keeping everyone law-abiding, in telling them not to fight. What is going to happen if they do fight?' 'Well', was the reply, in still kinder tones, 'if they fight that is their look-out. Too bad for them.' Dejectedly Malt said, 'I work hard to keep my people in order, and my name is good. I do not want people to speak my name and say, "Look, the people of Malt are fighting now" '. 'Oh, don't you worry', concluded the official. 'Your reputation isn't involved'.

---

1 Some of them had been jailed recently for brawling. They reminded themselves that the death of a recent Hagen councillor occurred during a land dispute.

2 I was also present. The conversation was in Pidgin.

This interchange is very revealing. The Administration official was speaking about the personal reputation which Malt had as a council member and which to his mind could not be affected by the behaviour of his tribesmen, who would suffer for their own faults. Although he did not voice this, he might have added that keeping his tribesmen in order was not really the councillor's job. Malt, on the other hand, felt that his reputation was bound up with this very thing. As he said on other occasions, a councillor is responsible for his people,[1] and what is his role if it is not to see that they keep the law? Councillors make rules at council meetings, they settle disputes, their whole work for the government is to bring government law to the people.

The two interpretations of the councillor's position on this occasion meant that the official could not communicate his sympathy nor the councillor his anxiety. Trivial as this incident was, the misunderstandings are central to the models which Hageners and many Administration officials entertain of their respective roles in the judicial system.

---

[1] And in many circumstances, this is the attitude of DDA. An official entry in the minutes of Dei Council for 1969 records the councillors being put to shame by a kiap for a homicide which occurred in their area. It ended: 'the government wants the trouble to end and does not want trouble to arise in this place', and suggested that the councillors themselves see to any issues over compensation.

Chapter 4

How the judicial system is perceived

> Yumi no inap kisim lo long han bilong yumi yet: we can't take the law into our own hands. (From a political education talk broadcast over Hagen radio, 1970)

> Kiap-nt kot tepa ik nimba lo pendepa wamb man ngomba etem e-mel ko unt na it: the kiap hears courts, has words to say, lays down laws, instructs people, and this is exactly what I used to do. (A former tultul recalling the days when he used to hear courts)

This chapter examines, first, differences between the models which Hageners and the Administration have of the judicial system, and, secondly, the notion of 'law', an important element in both models. When I refer in general to 'European' or 'Administration' attitudes I gloss over subtleties here in order to underline contrasts between the attitudes of Hageners and non-Hageners. Differences doubtless exist between the views of officials based in Port Moresby or on the spot in Mt Hagen, and between those who belong to DDA or the Department of Law,[1] but I do not give them detailed attention.

---

1. Recent events have highlighted some contrasts as they have been reported in the press. A European handed over compensation after a car accident, and the Post-Courier of 8 February 1972 noted, '[the] extortion payment in Mt Hagen has been described in legal circles as "a shocking and flagrant breach of the law" '. The following day (9 February 1972) it referred to the comments of a district officer, who 'said the Administration's attitude was that the payback business was nonsense and that it would eventually have to be cut out.... [But] a blending of the two cultures might be the first step - the people abiding by court decisions and regulations imposing a maximum ceiling on compensation prices'; and a local European businessman was reported as saying, 'We have dignified their customs through this ... and they have

I shall argue that although in a sense Hageners have assimilated a notion of 'law' and up to a point accept official dispute-settling agencies, their attitudes are based on a misunderstanding both of the structure of the judiciary and of some of its values. This misunderstanding is derived from the viewpoint of their own traditional judicial processes. One may also speak of a reciprocal misunderstanding on the part of many Europeans of what the Hagen viewpoint entails. This chapter will deal mainly with how the judicial structure is seen, who has what powers, how councillors and _komiti_ feel they fit in; while Chapter 5 turns to some of the assumptions lying behind the way in which Hageners 'use' the official courts and what they interpret to be the purpose of legal settlements.

Models

Hageners use the Pidgin word _kot_ ('court') freely.[1] It covers dispute-settling processes ranging from adjudication by the sub-district office, the welfare office or the Supreme Court to hearings which their own councillors and _komiti_ conduct. The term usually implies, however, some connection with the authority structure introduced by the Administration. It is not used much for private settlements agreed upon without recourse to councillor or _komiti_ or other officials.

Hageners visualise a hierarchy of officials: at the bottom are _komiti_ who handle minor issues; troublesome cases are referred to councillors, who in turn take matters too large for them to settle[2]

1 (continued)
dignified us...'. Again prominence (with picture coverage) was given by the _Post-Courier_ of 18 February 1972 to a peaceful monetary settlement of a dispute which had involved three deaths. 'Two patrol officers who had worked closely with the clans during the past two months played a major part in resolving the dispute.' The payments here would be between the tribes of the victims and murderers. The individuals who had actually committed the murders, however, were described by the Supreme Court (as reported on 10 February 1972) as 'primitive' men who 'had no sense of moral guilt'.

[1] In unofficial court procedure, councillors speak of 'holding' or 'hearing courts' (_kot tei, kot pili_), while a plaintiff says he 'will court [put a court on]' someone (_kot ndui_). The subject of dispute may also be a _kot_ ('There are two _kot_ [issues] here'), while a settlement is 'to have killed the _kot_'. 'Your _kot_ isn't straight', is said to someone who loses a case. A person who initiates a hearing is called 'the father [owner] of the _kot_'.

[2] Either because they prove difficult or because the trouble is classified as a grave one (see p.123). Councillors and _komiti_ apply to the Local Court, but do not go directly to the District Court.

to the police, kiap or LCM; these may themselves transfer cases to higher officials, including Supreme Court judges. ('If the matter does not go straight, then the kiap takes it to the big judge.') It is a continuum of process (the transfer of cases from one body to another) and also of authority, so that in this context councillors are seen as the immediate subordinates of kiap. (In other contexts they may claim equality or deny a ranking order.) The most important fact stemming from this perception is that, as far as settling disputes is concerned, councillors and komiti think they are acting as authorised deputies of the official magistrates.[1]

From the viewpoint of the Administration no such hierarchy exists. There is a sharp dividing line between local leaders who may take it on themselves to mediate in village disputes as a function of their general prominence, and persons with the authority of magistrates or judges who legally conduct judicial hearings. The powers bestowed on these persons are of a quite different order. Councillors by definition cannot hear courts and would be acting illegally to receive money payments after a successful mediation. In short, the official judiciary with its personnel having special entitlement to hear courts is qualitatively different from out-of-court settlement institutions - whereas a premise on which many councillors and komiti say they settle disputes is joint participation in a single system which embraces themselves, kiap and the Supreme Court bench.[2] I suggest this is one source for Hageners' acceptance of official dispute-settling agencies, their generally positive response to requests that certain matters should be taken to the police and so on, and a certain readiness to involve officials in their own disputes.

I have oversimplified the Administration model in one respect. Members of the Department of Law might draw a firmer line than members of DDA. In the 1960s cadet patrol officers were taught that they had an important role in settling complaints out of court, that encouragement should be given to the parties involved to reach their own solution, and that court action was a last resort. And while these complaints were called 'minor' it was also noted that they might cover not only civil but 'simple' criminal

---

[1] The authorisation element here should be stressed more than the subordination element, hence the term 'deputy'. These views are most characteristic of councillors near the town.

[2] For an example of a similar mode of thinking outside Papua New Guinea, see Fallers' discussion of official and unofficial courts in colonial Busoga (e.g., Fallers 1969:59).

matters as well.[1] Although in terms of authority a strong division is recognised between persons with different judicial qualifications, instructions of this kind reveal an administrative blurring in terms of jurisdiction, since they point to no simple equation between criminal offences for which court action is mandatory and civil actions which can be dealt with out of court.

The Hagen model is itself derived from several sources. First of all, councillors and komiti are seen as replacing former luluai and tultul, and Hageners believe that these persons were instructed to hold courts. Chapter 2 has described something of the perceived relationship between early village officials and kiap. The former regarded it as a central part of their duties to 'give law' to the people and it seems that they, along with locally stationed policemen, rapidly became personages to whom people would take their disputes. 'I was like a kiap and heard courts like a kiap', boasted one old tultul. The Kuma, eastern neighbours of Hageners, 'welcomed eagerly the informal courts which the Administration encouraged the luluais and tultuls to hold' (Reay 1964:246), and they 'received much informal training in the conduct of court cases' from their observation of hearings conducted by itinerant patrol officers. Berndt (1962) describes a similar situation in the Kainantu area, where even before luluai were appointed, embryonic courts arose under the stimulation of contact. These 'functioned simultaneously with traditional control mechanisms, being accepted as a congenial innovation in this field' (1962:314). Of that time (early 1950s) he writes (1962:383):

> In adopting the informal court, the eastern highlanders are accepting nothing which is not 'usable' within their own organisation and structure. In adapting it to their own use they do not seriously envisage it as serving the interests of the Administration.

Hageners, however, say that from the beginning village officials thought of themselves as doing the same work as kiap, and hence working with them to a common end. If this is no more than a recollection of the past, it still provides an ideological antecedent for the councillors' present position.

Many councillors and komiti today believe that the Administration expects them to settle disputes. Those acquainted with the

---

[1] From lecture notes issued by the then Department of Native Affairs as part of an induction course for cadet patrol officers at the Australian School of Pacific Administration.

terminology will call councillors' courts lokol kot,[1] and a councillor may open settlement proceedings by saying, 'I shall try this case in my lokol kot here before we think of taking it into town'. I have heard obedience to a summons from the Local Court in Mt Hagen being questioned on the grounds that a councillor's court would settle the issue just as well since it was after all a parallel authority: 'what is the court that we hear if it is not a lokol kot?' This particular incident occurred in the Dei Council area and an element here was the fact that the Local Court in Mt Hagen was seen as locally based, the appropriate agency within the council area being councillors' courts.[2] If this is an expression of independence from the centre, it is one based on an appropriation of powers by the periphery, in respect of a single system. There is widespread belief among komiti that government legislation permits them not only to suggest compensation payments but to derive monetary or other benefits from courts in reward for their work. And people may refuse the offer of a big-man or ex-village official to hear a court because this is properly the work of councillors and komiti. Sometimes the latter claim to have sent in reports of their court proceedings to the LCM and received his approval, in the same way that luluai were said to take reports to the kiap.

One source for this notion lies in the ideology that councillors and komiti administer the same law as Administration officials; another source lies in the direct comparison of the office of councillor or komiti with that of kiap. Councillor Malt,[3] in speaking abstractly of his duties, said (to me), 'Mi bihainim laik bilong ol kiap tasol, i no laik bilong mi (I follow the wishes of the kiap, not my own inclination); I just think of following the law book [regulations and ordinances] and hold courts. If I were to make things up, people would feel it wasn't right and go and ask the government, and the government would say, "What kind of a councillor is he?"' On another occasion, at a court hearing over a divorce, he proclaimed that he was a worthy councillor who heard everyone's courts and did not single out anyone for special help, because he dispensed government law.

---

[1] One councillor explained the contrast between 'local' and 'district' courts as being between those a councillor hears and those brought by the police.

[2] That is, Local Courts were the concern of particular council areas, as the District Court was the concern of the District. It would also be felt appropriate that cases should be heard by the LCM on circuit at the Dei Council chambers - rather than in another council area - or else be taken to the Dei Council kiap.

[3] See pp.113ff.

Were he to trick people he would lose at the next election, so that the only course of action he could take (em wanpela rot bilong mi - he gave emphasis to this by speaking Pidgin) was to act fairly. Again, a komiti reported that a policeman upheld one of his (the komiti's) decisions with the words, 'It is the law of the kiap which the komiti takes, it isn't another law that he administers at home'. (According to the same man's account, this policeman recommended that a compensation pig be eaten by the komiti's kot.) In referring to the 'law', then, people often think of it as 'the law which the kiap dispenses'.

There are several facets to the way in which councillors and komiti regard themselves as linked to kiap. Initially 'kiap' referred only to DDA officers, but the model has expanded with the influx of new officials. The Local Court Magistrate can be known as kiap,[1] as are police officers, and comparisons are extended to them. Thus spoke komiti Karingk[2] during a dispute between a father, son and daughter-in-law: 'I, I hold the law here (na ya lo tep mor); and I hear the talk all of you have made. I am just like a police officer (kundi plis), and I can listen to all your troubles.' A linking concept here is the double equation, first between councillors and big-men, secondly between big-men and kiap. A detailed examination of this is given by A.J. Strathern, who argues (1970:549) that kiap 'have been taken as something of a model for authoritative behaviour by councillors ... although few councillors behave in ways that closely resemble those of the kiaps'.

Like traditional big-men, the kiap is seen to have a multi-functional role, and the role of councillor is interpreted in the same way. Dispute-settling was clearly a function of the early kiap but so was keeping law and order in a wider sense. It is regarded as appropriate for councillors to make speeches on what they see as social problems: for example, a rising divorce rate, increasing waywardness in women, and (until recent council rules came into force) spiralling bridewealths. The kiap, it was said, decided there should be councillors and komiti so that people would not steal and generally make trouble. It is indeed the authoritative powers of the kiap which are crucial to the model, and councillors constantly complain of those who do not follow their advice (ol bikhet man). But in the same way as ordinary men always had the possibility of establishing relations with a

---

[1] And I have heard this from the mouth of an ADC. One ex-komiti explained to me, 'The judge is a kiap, but they call him judge'. Ofisa is occasionally used for kiap, LCM or police officer. (Mihalic 1971:366 translates magistrate as kiap.)

[2] See p.90.

big-man, so many people feel that they can bypass councillors and on their own tap higher sources of power. In their terms, it needs 'strength' to do this successfully. Such action does not so much deny the hierarchy as demonstrate that some individuals have the power to jump certain of its rungs. Hence appeals may be made directly to kiap or the police. Councillors often openly resent such behaviour, stating that the proper procedure would be to bring issues to themselves in the first instance.

Councillors and komiti are equated verbally with kiap, perhaps with a distinguishing marker, as in møi keap ('home [lit. 'earth'] kiap'). A councillor may refer to himself as a masta. One young thief, describing how he shared the meat of a stolen pig with his clan mates, added that he would not, of course, give any to the komiti of the clan: komiti are like kiap, he said, they have put a law against stealing. An ex-luluai, referring to the efforts of a councillor and several komiti in trying to suggest a suitable award in one case, urged the disputants to listen to their words because, in the persons of the councillor and komiti, 'a big kiap has come' - these men were only doing what a kiap would do and the disputants could not behave as though kiap had never come to Hagen.

Among factors which perpetuate Hageners' belief that the hearing of courts by councillors has official approval is constant emphasis from kiap that they should settle minor disputes themselves. Something about this has already been said in Chapter 3. Thus council minutes record advisers recommending that councillors and komiti should settle 'small' troubles quickly before they develop into 'big' ones, or that only 'big' troubles should be brought to the Local Court. The use of 'big' and 'small' in this context is revealingly ambiguous. The words can be interpreted as pointing either to disparity or to continuity. To the adviser, the contrast may well be between criminal action where the law has been infringed, and civil squabbles that are best left to the people to decide upon for themselves: in the same way as a person might privately take a dispute in Australia to an arbitrator, said one kiap to me. I have already noted the tendency for some kiap at least to equate civil issues with petty if not trivial complaints.[1] To his hearers, 'big' and 'small' may simply underline the continuum they feel exists between issues they handle themselves and those they call in outsiders to deal with ('If we cannot settle it, we take it to the kiap, and if he says it is a big court, then he takes it to the big judge'). 'Bigness' here may refer either to the difficulty of a case (it is hard to settle) or to its gravity in terms of the types of issues in which people

---

[1] And see the reasons for referral mentioned in Chapter 3 (p.86).

know different authorities are interested. Thus I was told at Kelua that it was mandatory to take homicides at once to the police or the kiap because everyone would be afraid lest fighting broke out. Although there is certainly a notion that the kinds of cases in which the official authorities are most interested are important ('big') because of their implications for keeping the peace, and these especially include crimes of violence, Hageners certainly do not gloss over the cases which it is recommended they deal with themselves - concerning pigs, women, debts - as trivial.[1] Matters which the plis kot pursues (drunkenness, card-playing) often seem less important than their courts over bridewealth and divorce. These kinds of cases are 'small' only in the sense that they fall firmly within the competence of councillors and komiti,[2] who, with emphatic official encouragement, try to settle them rather than refer them immediately to the Administration. They are certainly not 'small' in terms of social importance, or 'private' in a European sense. 'Private' issues would never go as far as the councillor.

Councillors and komiti also agree with the expressed European view that they are more competent than outsiders to deal with matters of local custom. A councillor must be someone, people say, who knows both the ways of white men and the ways of the ancestors. At a public meeting held in the Dei Council area in 1964, one councillor explained that the kiap had found it necessary to create councillors because he himself could not handle people who were persistent trouble-makers - those who stole pigs and sugarcane all the time.

In this context one might also add that councillors at council meetings often complain of the way people 'bighead'. An adviser, thinking perhaps mainly of the councillors' administrative functions, may say, 'If you work hard, then everyone must listen to what you have to say'; but this can be interpreted as encouragement for all councillor activities, including that of dispute-settling. Advisers are also quoted as saying that komiti are like policemen to the councillors, and for the work they do they should be supported by the people, that is, have their gardens made and houses built by them.

---

[1] Disputes concerning women may be called trivial, but this dogma is belied by the amount of time and energy which goes into settling them. It is a dogma that has more to do with the status of women than with notions of judicial importance.

[2] That is, where councillors politely agree it is appropriate that they deal with 'small' matters, this is a comment on the respective status of themselves and the kiap, rather than on the significance of the cases with which they deal.

The result of the Hagen viewpoint is that councillors and *komiti* take on themselves 'duties' they have no legal right to perform (settling criminal matters, imposing fine-like payments),[1] while the official tendency to dismiss councillors' courts as 'private mediations' leads to an underestimation by Europeans of their law-keeping functions.

Administration officials may call dispute-settlement a waste of councillors' time because it disrupts other activities, such as roadwork. *Kiap* and the LCM deny that people bring to them fine money (in the same way as the issue of canes to *luluai* and *tultul* is denied). Some Europeans regard the use of money or valuables in the settling of grievances as 'mercenary', and suggest that a person allowed to 'get away with' paying compensation escapes punishment altogether. 'I would not encourage a councillor to settle a theft case himself', I was told, 'because then the person does not get to [the Local] Court and is therefore not punished'.[2] The same speaker (a member of DDA) also suggested that it was actually against a councillor's own interests to involve himself in arbitration in case unpopular decisions jeopardised his election chances. Another official (from the Department of Law) suggested that compensation payments as recommended by councillors were really just excuses for feasts, that councillors extracted what they could for themselves out of disputes, and that their 'courts' were rackets to fleece people. He cited adultery settlements as an example of corruption: councillors, he said, simply persuade the guilty man to hand over the largest pig he has, and then they eat it themselves. The husband gets no satisfaction. So even by their own customs they are not doing the right thing, since the wronged man is not compensated.[3] His main objection against councillors hearing cases was that they might take too much into their hands and deal with criminal matters without regard to the due processes of law. 'What happens to the innocent man or woman?' he asked. 'For no-one ever gets off when they are

---

[1] See Nash (1970) who points out that under present ordinances many Papua New Guinean group (business) enterprises are probably illegal associations.

[2] Punishment was always a component of traditional compensation procedures (Chapter 1).

[3] A pig was a traditional item given as compensation for adultery in the past. Hageners regard the husband as satisfied with an arrangement whereby the guilty man hands over an item, whether or not he (the husband) subsequently decides to share the animal with his clansmen. Sometimes several items are handed over, and the husband retains one for himself; occasionally he decides not to share anything.

accused by a councillor.' He did, however, go on to compare councillors with Justices of the Peace, who are essentially untrained men. Interestingly enough, the basis for his comparison was in power terms: JPs are men of substance, he pointed out, middle or upper-middle class, and councillors hold positions of power, too. He supposed that councillors enjoyed using their power and that their role in mediations was part of this. In other words, his view was that councillors hold hearings in order to extract wealth from village people and increase their general standing.

In all these statements from Europeans, we find the suggestion that because unofficial courts are no more than forums for informal mediation, they are not only illegal where they act beyond their domain of competence, but are also 'non-legal' phenomena. That is, where they are not concerned with trivial, domestic issues, they deal with matters which are really local politics and rely on making adjustments through bargaining much as industrial arbitration tribunals do.[1] They are therefore far removed from proper legal institutions such as courts.[2]

There is a parallel between the way Administration officials regard councillors and komiti and the way these persons see themselves in relation to ordinary people. The Administration teaches that self-help must be abandoned, that people should not take the law into their own hands. Councillors' attempts to deal with criminal matters may be seen by officials as flagrant breaches of this principle, whereas councillors think they are preventing the disputants from doing precisely this.

Understanding procedure

Since they regard their own councillors and komiti as acting 'in' rather than 'out of' court, it is not surprising that Hageners usually misunderstand the relationship between the police and

---

1 Cf. Epstein (1970b:55-6) on a point which (he suggests) worries many lawyers in Papua New Guinea: that because a dispute has been settled through procedures which take into account the social distance between the litigants this means the abandonment of any attempt to administer the law as such. He writes (1970b:56): 'however obvious the political aspects of a dispute, the battle itself is waged through the marshalling of arguments, all of which have their basis in the customary law of the people'. Kaberry (1941-42:350) makes a similar point: 'rights are asserted and an appeal made to ... standards of conduct'.

2 Some theorists writing on law separate 'legal' from 'political' processes. For recent critiques see Moore (1970), Fallers (1969:ch.1).

judiciary on the one hand and informal arbitration or mediation agencies on the other. In Chapter 3 I described the network of extra-curial bodies which become involved in settling civil disputes. Often Hageners treat this network as though it also had hierarchical aspects. Perhaps the most powerful aspect of their own model (a hierarchy of personnel dealing with difficult issues) is that it carries with it an idea of delegated authority (from highest to lowest), which provides a set of sanctions (a councillor can threaten to take a matter to a higher person who will support his judgment). As I mention in Chapter 5, the whole question of sanctions is an important one in councillors' eyes. A result is that when any outside agent is called in he may be expected to deliver the kinds of authoritative judgments which are delivered in the official courts.

The official distinction between criminal and civil offences is blurred in another way. If, in taking civil disputes to outsiders, Hageners hope for a firm application of rules and principles as are emphatically laid down in criminal cases, so also are criminal offences often treated by them as though they were civil ones. By this I mean that the process of prosecution through court channels is often regarded as a strategy in disputes between individuals. Hageners appreciate that the 'law' or the 'court' deals with offenders because the offender has infringed rules, but it was always the case that in traditional dispute-settlement appeals would be made to community values and principles of conduct, and these could be held separate from the fact that particular individuals were injured. Through the Local Court a plaintiff may see himself as initiating an official record of an issue, bringing in the sanctions of the police and a court process, and then winning or losing the case. Although he may receive no personal benefit, and although in the eyes of the court the case is framed as an issue between the criminal and the state, the plaintiff may regard it as an issue between himself and the defendant.[1] On this premise, the adversary context of the Supreme Court is not always intelligible. The Hagen focus for contest is the relationship between victim and wrong-doer. In traditional procedures it was usually fairly clear which rules had been infringed, which values ignored, and Hageners belittle the official effort to explore precisely in what ways laws may have been broken.

The following minor points of procedure in the workings of the Local Court are probably obscure to many Hageners. (i) A defendant's rights in relation to the different jurisdictions

---

[1] And doubtless this is true of many cases that go through Australian courts as well.

of the Local or District Court, and rights of appeal: they may regard a court as being satisfactory or not, but the idea that the law can be badly administered is not so easily grasped. (ii) The invitation to speak on oath: this is usually explained to the defendant in terms of the weight his words will carry (rather than in terms of sanctions as is the case in their own oath procedures, e.g., 'if you lie, God will kill you'), and most Hageners probably think that truth is something for the magistrate to assess. It is his job to catch the defendant out if he is lying. The apparent acceptance of a defendant's statements by a magistrate can be puzzling: a man may plead guilty, but present a plausible case in the hope of a light sentence. Spectators sometimes wonder why words appear to be taken at face value and why there is so little attention to the verbal arts. (iii) Defendants are allowed to suggest factors which might mitigate sentence, but the question is sometimes interpreted as offering a choice of penalties or as a demand for a further admission of guilt ('Yes, I should be punished'). (iv) Litigants are not always clear at what points in the proceedings they are required to speak out fully or answer only in direct response to questions, and may be criticised by a magistrate for speaking at the wrong time or for not having taken the chance to speak at the right time. (v) Bail is regarded as being related to whether a court is won or lost (whether the bail money is returned or not), but at the time of its imposition may simply be accepted as a payment to the court. (A single Pidgin term, <u>baim ofis</u> (Mihalic 1971: 364-5), is used generally for both 'bail' and 'court fine', and Hageners speak of <u>baim kot</u> in the same way.) (vi) A person who does not appear at the court at the precise moment when his name is called may still think he can present his case later, as was always possible in the <u>kiap</u>'s court. (vii) The Local Court's emphasis on individual responsibility and criminal intention, a point to which I return in Chapter 5.

On the other hand, other aspects are understood fairly clearly. (i) Taking a trouble case to the adjudication of someone with the power to impose penalties. (ii) The basic purpose of the Local Court in bringing crimes to light and punishing offenders. (iii) Its requirement of formality in the behaviour of the litigants towards the magistrate (the former should speak only at certain times, be respectful, appear on the day summoned). (iv) The importance of witnesses in contested cases. (v) Court fines as well as jail sentences constituting punishment. (vi) The police support of court orders. There are also areas of ambiguity. These include the total functions of the Local Court, the amount of information acceptable as evidence in a hearing, what admission to guilt means,[1] the precise powers of the police, magistrates and other personnel, and, as I have already mentioned, their out-of-court roles. Some of these points I return to again later.

Understanding law

In Hagen usage lo refers to many things. There are three salient clusters of meaning: (i) specific rules (laws), (ii) modes of conduct (orderly or lawful behaviour), and (iii) a modern style of life ('rule of law').

Specific rules include the edicts of particular persons such as kiap, as well as council recommendations and resolutions, and orders about conduct laid down by the House of Assembly. There is obviously an overlap between offences as Hageners traditionally classified them and those expressly forbidden in regulations and ordinances. In councillors' courts, the most overt references are made to laws having been broken when these derive from relatively novel injunctions (e.g., that weapons should not be carried in public) or where there has been physical assault or some other violence. This partly echoes what is known to be an official preoccupation with crimes of violence. At the same time references to 'broken laws' may reinforce expressed disapproval of acts condemned on a whole range of traditional grounds, or be a weapon of abuse in the hands of the litigants ('You are the kind of man who breaks laws!').

Councillors for a long time imagined that one of their functions was to draw up 'laws' at council meetings, and both Hagen and Dei Councils were concerned during the 1960s with the need to frame legislation on problems (as the male councillors saw them) relating to bridewealth, divorce, and control of sexual promiscuity in women.[2] They also regarded themselves as being able to modify 'government law' (and council minutes record the kiap asking councillors about their opinion of present laws dealing with such topics as adultery). Litigants during a dispute may be asked sarcastically by a councillor or komiti if they think they can go their own way rather than heed the authority of the men who really make laws: 'Are you making a new law just for yourself, then?'.

---

[1] The early records show most pleas recorded by Hageners were 'guilty', but this is changing now, and an increasing number of 'not guilty' pleas are made.

[2] Many council 'resolutions' are lo in this sense but only a very few ever receive official ratification.

Apart from substantive rules (injunctions, regulations) there are also procedural rules. Lo can refer to the principles by which a kiap or LCM settles a case. These may be enunciated directly by the official or be deduced from his behaviour. Precedents are established during the court process, and disputants may argue among themselves because they are uncertain of what the current lo is on such-and-such a matter - since they cannot recall a recent case being taken to the Local Court which dealt with the concatenation of issues now facing them. It is in this context that Hageners often talk of 'new laws coming up', by which they mean changes in the emphasis which different magistrates and other people give in their settlements. There are often drastic contrasts, for example, in the way various officials handle marriage disputes or pig trespass. In 1970 men at Kelua attempted to work out ways in which to deal with several incidents of pigs breaking into gardens according to what they interpreted as new injunctions from kiap - that garden produce was more important than pigs and that it would therefore be right to shoot pigs at sight (rather than putting the onus on the gardener to fence his land properly). 'There are many lo [processes by which we can reach settlement]', commented a komiti during an intractable slander case, and this an observer glossed for my benefit as referring to the fact that 'the laws of the kiap' constantly alter, in the same way (he added) as women are always changing their minds. A kiap's personal emphasis on imposing jail sentences or on demanding large or small fines is thus 'his' lo. In 1970, again, people in one council area were discussing the 'new laws' of their council president: high rates of compensation that he had said should be paid in cases of theft to discourage the stealing that was becoming so prevalent. ('P [the president] told the other councillors, and they put this lo ... and the kiap followed his talk and said it was good, and if P's group humbugged with him he could carry this out.')

Finally, the whole process by which disputes are settled may be referred to as lo, so that a person who has no 'road' or 'way' (nombokla) to escape responsibility for his acts 'has no lo'.

The lo of this first cluster of meanings specifies certain regulations and processes that must be adhered to if law and order is to be maintained; but the concept of law and order itself is more embracing. Lo in the sense of orderly behaviour, a style of conduct, approaches the European concept of 'law and order', though it has a significant twist to it. Law and order is sometimes regarded by Administration officials as something to be imposed, and in the early days when pacification of warring tribes was being carried out, order was very definitely a matter of establishing control. In appealing to people to settle differences without recourse to violence, however, the Administration could draw to some extent, knowingly or not, on traditional notions surrounding peaceable settlement and the ideology of reconciliation.[1] A Hagen gloss of 'law and order' would probably not only embrace peaceful behaviour, but also peaceful intentions. ('Now is the time of lo and why should I lie to you!' exclaimed one orator during a heated altercation.) When councillors and komiti settle issues they look for evidence that the litigants no longer harbour feelings of revenge. This partly explains why they tend to be so sensitive over matters apparently trivial but ones which can give some insight into the state of mind of an aggrieved person. Unofficial courts provide a context in which such feelings can be expressed, although they are not always successful in channelling them. The physical retaliation which Yuimb[2] took after the attack on his pig was criticised by one komiti because Yuimb had 'cut the law' - acted out his feelings of revenge instead of working towards a peaceable solution.

During the poison confrontation,[3] disputants made innumerable references to the fact that they were 'men of lo' and would not therefore handle poison, or accuse others wrongly, as the case might be. The protest was not simply that they had not done something but that they would have had no such intention. Whatever actual feelings existed, honesty of motive was one of the issues which had to be declared publicly. Countless speeches reiterated the theme:

> Before we fought but that is a long time over. I was a fighting man but now I am old. You are all new men here, and a good lo has come up and now we sit down on top of it.... You are making all these accusations, but what would the people you accuse be angry about that you think they would send you poison?

This leads to the third cluster of meanings. Here lo means 'custom' rather than 'orderly behaviour'. People may say, 'This is our lo', in reference to traditional ways of dealing with certain troubles, and contrast 'custom' (lo) with lo kopa ('true

---

[1] Early patrol reports give evidence of the rapidity with which newly contacted Hageners accepted 'courts', so that initial patrols into an area were able to 'settle disputes'. Modern people may be compared favourably (by Hageners) with their ancestors as being persons 'who have good talk to say'.

[2] See Case 3, pp.38-40.

[3] See Case 5, pp.100-3.

[authorised] law') - ratified council rulings or government legislation. Or they may contrast lo, the modern style of life, with pasin (Pidgin for Melpa ukl, 'custom'), life as their ancestors knew it. For Hageners see themselves (not all of the time) as having been transformed by the arrival of Europeans and as living under the dispensation of lo. This is linked to notions of advancement, progress, development and business enterprise. It has some affinities with the concept of 'the rule of law'.[1] In giving it emphasis, Hageners and Europeans alike overdramatise previous 'lawlessness'.[2] This equates the unquestionable fact that there have been radical changes since the arrival of Europeans with the introduction of new lo in the first two senses.

Although people often describe various changes in terms of progress ('White men have come, lo has come up and the kiap shows us the road to business'),[3] there are ambiguities in their statements as well. For example, they may distinguish not between the ways of their ancestors and the way things have been since white men first arrived, but between life as it was under the old luluai and tultul and as it is now under councillors and komiti. Here lo refers to the whole structure of elections and paid office, to a new leniency they perceive in the way councillors and magistrates deal with offenders, as well as to increasing material comforts and monetary wealth. A councillor from Dei Council who had assisted early patrols spoke of how then the kiap made everyone work hard as labourers, and how village officials expended effort in forcing people to comply with the demands of the new regime, and how then there were no rewards for such works. Labourers were paid with newspaper and tobacco and there was no money about: 'Before we worked hard', he commented, 'but now a good lo has come up'. A minor big-man from near Mt Hagen, recalling the time when he was jailed by the CNA (about 1957) for what he claims was a mistaken accusation of adultery, said:

> No-one listened to me - they all helped the woman. Nowadays we hear courts and take notice of what is said, but before the bosboi and luluai didn't follow lo, they just jailed me.[4] Now we get to the bottom

---

1 For example, Smithers (1965).

2 Cf. Epstein (1970b:55).

3 The particular speaker was referring to the comments he had heard from a kiap to the effect that troubles and fighting hindered economic development; but much vaguer links are also made between 'law' and 'business'.

4 His case was brought to the attention of the court by a luluai.

> of troubles, but at that time many of us didn't know Pidgin and the *kiap* didn't understand well. The *kiap* didn't listen to talk - if a man was in trouble he was jailed.

The 'new law' (*lo kont*) can thus refer either to all the changes there have been under Australian peace, so that *luluai* are recalled as having 'given law' to previously warring groups ('opening up the place', *kona para ndui*, a phrase also used of settling troubles through 'good words' rather than fighting), or alternatively *lo* has really only come recently (*akopi mint lo ekit onom*, 'only now has it come outside [among us]') since the abolition of *luluai* and their rights to inflict physical punishment upon offenders and beat them with canes. Whichever position is stressed, it is clear that a salient idea is the progressive weakening of physical sanctions in the hands of Hageners, with increasing reliance on settling issues through talking in courts.

Old men sometimes speak sarcastically of the 'softening' there has been. For the paradox is that while in one sense (clusters i and iii) people nowadays know about *lo*, in another sense they are actually more prone to lawless behaviour (cluster ii). Hageners state this clearly: 'Since the banning of warfare we have *lo* but there is more humbug too', or '*Luluai* and *tultul* were strong, and the *kiap* told them to beat people, but now *lo* has come up we can't do this and people humbug'. From here it is only one step to other comments one also hears which expressly voice apprehensiveness about the *lo*.

> When *lo* [the future] finally comes up and our children are all at school, we shall be ruined. Now we are still all right, we still follow some of the ways of our ancestors - but what will happen when *lo* comes and we have to buy everything with money?[1]

Often this is directly linked to the fact that councillors cannot appear to act as authoritatively as *luluai* and *tultul* did, for they do not command the same range of sanctions. This problem has long vexed councillors: at the seventh meeting of Mt Hagen Council in 1962 questions were already being raised over the powers they had. In the words of one ex-*luluai*:

> When I was a *luluai* people did not fight; they lived quietly, and did government work.... *Komiti* and councillors do not hear courts properly, and nowadays

---

[1] The speaker was among the first of his tribe to experience paid employment with Europeans, and has been consistently involved in business enterprises.

> people get into trouble. They buy commercial vehicles, travel about in them, seduce women, go to bars and drink, then get worked up and men get killed by the cars or are angry over the seductions and they drink more, and fights develop.... Before when women left their husbands and were a nuisance I would beat them and after that they would settle down. In all the courts I heard I never divorced anyone. But now councillors have come they break marriages, and women go off from one man to another. In the past I would give such a woman a beating, and then bring her before the kiap, and she would behave after that.... Before I was strong, my head had power [he used the Pidgin word pawa]. My work was strong - not like that of the councillors. Shall I come back and take up my work again?

These three clusters of meanings of lo derive partly from teachings of the Administration. Hageners have been forced to acknowledge the applicability of certain rules; to abandon warfare and observe more restraints on violent behaviour than in the past; and to recognise that along with economic development, law is one of the benefits which European rule has brought them. Yet all three have little bearing on law in the sense in which kiap use it when they dismiss the possibility of councillors hearing courts as 'unlawful'. Law in this sense refers to a constitutional arrangement whereby the authority to act in certain ways is allocated among a number of offices. Within the judiciary, only specified persons may hold courts. As we have seen, the Hagen model of the authority structure is very different. It would be fair to say that few Hageners appreciate the legal (constitutional) relationships between kiap, Local Court Magistrates, the police and so on. Their own perception is in terms of functions (which kinds of troubles particular officials deal with) and of power (the relative sanctions at their disposal). Legality in this context is obscure to them. It is also probably the case that lo in all of the Hageners' senses is obscure to some Europeans.

Chapter 5

The working of the system

> [The law] has to change with the times as social environment changes. Any society gets the government, police force and law it deserves. (Secretary for Law as quoted in Post-Courier, 3 December 1971)

> A villager is not judged from his intrinsic worth as an uneducated man possessing his own traditional concepts of justice, morality and sense of law and order. Instead he is often judged from the exterior, a man who must be taught to abide by the law... (Sakora 1970:17)

Hageners regard their courts as part of the official judiciary, and say that councillors and komiti are like kiap. But if we look at the functioning and aims of the official and unofficial courts we find several significant differences, in the same way as the powers and activities of kiap make them behave in very different ways from councillors.[1]

The particular Hagen model I have described pastes over these discrepancies. It is pertinent to ask why, in a society lacking developed notions of rank, with no indigenous hierarchy of office-holders, a conceptual hierarchy of this kind should hold any attraction. The answer revolves around the facts of power. Europeans imposed themselves through using force and maintained their position in the early years by direct resort to physical sanctions. Hageners were impelled to accept the physical superiority of kiap. The image of the powerful, arbitrary kiap, who yet referred to abstract precepts ('the law') and said he was doing things for people's own good, echoed some elements, though only some, of the characteristics of the big-man. Big-men appear to have been eager

[1] A number of points in this chapter are derived from discussions with Andrew Strathern, and accounts given in A.J. Strathern (1972b) and (in press) are relevant here.

to meet the challenge. This they did by appropriating the authority of the newcomers. The hierarchical model envisages a chain of personnel down which strength is passed, so that the power and authority of *kiap* can be tapped. I have already noted that Hageners frequently apply the model to include agencies which mediate in civil disputes, as when they try to use persons in this network as though they too were ordered hierarchically. They look to a man such as the welfare officer for stronger decisions than he can or wants to make. This is a kind of feedback process. For what the chain-of-personnel notion provides are sanctions at the disposal of councillors and *komiti*. Officials are often appealed to merely in order to demonstrate that these sanctions exist. There is an anomaly (for Hageners) in the idea of officials with advice or recommendations to give but no sanctions of their own.

To follow van Velsen (1969), it would perhaps be analytically proper to compare councillors and *komiti* not with magistrates at court sittings, but with the *kiap*, LCM and others in their non-magisterial roles as out-of-court mediators. This is what the Administration model does. But in effect much of the authority which such mediators have for Hageners lies in the fact that the latter do not clearly discriminate between the separate powers of these officials but attribute a general power to them all. Mediation may be successful to a European because it is removed from a court context; to a Hagener it may be successful precisely because of its approximation to a court process. Hence councillors and *komiti* regard themselves, and act accordingly, as though they, too, were operating Administration sanctions (jail, calling in police) more automatically than they possibly can. Councillors will say to someone not heeding their words: 'You realise that if you "bighead" with us you are really "bigheading" with the *kiap*'. They quote the LCM as saying that if people do not agree to their recommendations, councillors should bring them in and he would deal with them himself, or they report that the LCM fines people for being 'bigheads'. A defendant who refuses to come to an unofficial court is a 'bighead', exactly as is someone who fails to appear before a *kiap* on a census patrol. For given that many councillors take their court-hearing roles seriously, the nature of the sanctions they wield is of the utmost importance to them.[1]

---

[1] This seems to be true throughout the Western Highlands (see, e.g., Colebatch *et al* (1971:221)). Hide (1971) describes how members of land demarcation committees in Chimbu in 1967 felt that in order to hear 'land courts' they needed some authority through which they could enforce their decisions. P. Brown (1963:11) records the plea of an Eastern Highlands councillor that laws should be made so that people would listen to what councillors had to say.

And it is Administration reluctance to endow councillors and komiti with official judicial authority which lies at the heart of the misunderstandings that exist.

Adaptations

Kiap and full-time magistrates, such as the LCM, handle court cases rather differently, but as the more familiar figure the kiap remains the chief referent in Hagen thinking. However, in the vicinity of the town one may find points of procedure in the unofficial courts which particularly echo those of the Local Court as heard by the LCM. In Case 6, for example,[1] the komiti said he had asked the complainant under whose jurisdiction he would like the case to be heard. Direct statements may be made as to how the komiti thinks the LCM would hear a plea,[2] as well as a more general mention of what a kiap's attitude would be on a particular issue (as in Case 2).[3] This last case shows how such references may be used as tools of persuasion: on the one hand, the implicit threat in the councillor's references to the kiap was that he (the councillor) felt his position strong enough to take the case to officials, while on the other hand, since the point of discussion was an issue towards which it was known kiap were sceptical, the councillor could present the threat in terms of a challenge to official attitudes. But the same message was conveyed, that he was arguing from a strong position. Finally, in Case 5[4] we saw procedural principles being used as direct weapons with which to belabour opponents.

An important function which reference to procedure has in all these instances is to invest the councillor's hearing with a semblance both of authority (he is acting with the approval of the kiap) and of power (he can coerce the disputants into accepting his recommendations, as officials do). In reality, councillors and komiti still basically negotiate rather than adjudicate in matters of dispute. They have to fall back on the kinds of constraints which were effective in the past - pointing out the value of paying compensation, shaming offenders, thoroughly publicising causes of grievances, threatening more unpleasant reactions from others. And in appealing to points of procedure they are not merely following a set routine but trying to strengthen their bargaining position.

---

[1] See p.106.

[2] See Case 1, p.28.

[3] See p.32.

[4] See p.100.

Notice of official procedure has also introduced some real modifications into dispute-settlement. There has been a considerable carry-over from traditional peaceable settlement procedure, so much so that I would call the unofficial courts 'neotraditional', to use Fallers' phrase (Fallers 1969), rather than 'innovatory'. Nevertheless, proceedings are much more formal than they ever were in the past. 'To court someone' before a councillor or komiti sets in train a relatively predictable series of events. People are able to 'report' matters to these persons in a way that was not feasible with traditional big-men. Conversely komiti also expect to be listened to when they make recommendations. Overworked komiti also have an interest in restricting discussions, which they do by perhaps refusing to reopen a case[1] which has already been publicly 'settled', or threatening to abandon the whole proceedings, or taking the matter to a higher official when disputants will not agree to agree. They sometimes see themselves in situations where it is their duty to prevent recourse to violence (Case 8); so that the kinds of satisfactions which litigants can derive from unofficial courts have definite limits.

Komiti take on themselves the task of administering punishment, although physical punishment is rare except in cases where women are involved. Imposing payment, as we have seen, may be interpreted as punishing the defendant. Conscious effort is made to have the principals on both sides brought together, although the interpretation of who constitute the principals to a dispute might not follow official thinking.[2] Possibly more scrupulous attention is paid to evidence in those cases which in the past would have led to minor fighting or brawling. Certainly the role of 'witness' is nowadays formalised to the extent that persons who choose to act as witnesses[3] see themselves not only as providing evidence which may or may not help the litigants but as being partly responsible for the results of their revelations. More weight, also, is possibly given nowadays to the punitive element in compensation payments - partly because this is replacing punitive measures that before took other forms, such as violent retaliation. The 'new laws' introduced by one council president[4] to discourage thieving recommended compensation payments of a crippling magnitude: a thief who stole a pig would have to find not just one or two in return but ten, whereas the rates for

---

[1] This is regarded as one of the 'laws of kiap'.

[2] In a case of adultery between two married people, for example, the wife of the adulterous husband would be most unlikely to be treated as having a formal complaint to make.

[3] See Cases 6 and 7 and the discussion on pp.106-7.

[4] See p.131.

thefts of peanuts were advertised as £5[1] (instead of $1 or so), of sweet potatoes £5, and of bananas or sugarcane $4 the first time and a pig the second time.

Traditional elements persist in the notion that councillors and komiti have an authority to handle disputes since they are in a more general sense political leaders (as kiap were at the sub-district level in the past). Because of their personal influence they stand some chance of succeeding in an appeal to norms and values, thereby overriding tendencies towards autonomy on the part of disputants. (It is also true, however, that political leaders who do not bear the title of councillor or komiti are not formally approached to settle matters.) Compensation procedures, the rules of which are universally understood, also provide an extremely important framework within which councillors and komiti strive to achieve settlement, and reference to liability to pay compensation can be used as a sanction over a whole range of issues, from quarrels between kinsmen to flagrant assault. Recommendations in terms of payments indicate judgment: where the blame lies, who should be punished, whether the disputants should make an attempt at reconciliation, and so on. But since they also allow, if need be, for judgment to be implicit rather than explicit,[2] settlement can be achieved to the satisfaction of the plaintiff without the defendant losing too much face. Indeed, I have already noted that through a generous payment the defendant may recover self-esteem. Also crucial to what Hageners expect from courts is the time which komiti will give to disputants who wish to talk out an issue, and their recognition of the necessity of getting to the 'root of the trouble'. A case may be more or less settled through confessions alone, so that final judgments of guilt which might give rise to further grievances are evaded. To this end a councillor or komiti will make use of all the information he has at his disposal. In order to assess what kind of procedure will make for the most satisfactory outcome (to openly place or not to place blame, for example), he needs to be aware not only of the facts of the dispute but its background, and this may range from details of domestic history to the state of political relations. Although councillors see themselves as 'impartial', this is based on a premise of intention ('You all know what kinds of interest I might have in this case, but for the purpose of getting this dispute settled, I am not going to help either side: so you can heed my

---

[1] People use pounds (£) and dollars ($) interchangeably in reference to Australian currency. I quote the figures as they were told to me.

[2] See Case 7, pp.107-8.

decision') rather than status ('I have no interest at all in this case: so you can heed my decision'). From such a point of view, having foreknowledge of a case is far from a disqualification, and indeed Hageners are sometimes puzzled by the fact that the LCM so obviously restricts himself to the information persons choose to place before him. Komiti encourage people to bring to them reports[1] of troubles as they arise, so that should courts later be held they will already know how some of the participants stand on various issues. Constant accessibility is one of the chief services which councillors, and to a greater extent komiti, offer. This in itself marks their position off from that of the kiap or LCM. Komiti cannot put many restrictions on the time they make available to hearing complaints and may be approached in all circumstances and at all hours. Finally, the competence of a komiti to hear a case is not circumscribed solely in terms of the authorisation he is seen to derive from the official judiciary: he must have a fine knowledge of customary ways of dealing with disputes and is explicitly required by people to make adjustments between traditional and introduced values. He thus all the time has to refer, however implicitly, to 'custom' - either because it is appropriate or in explanation of why it is not appropriate. And because of his position as negotiator he has to be much more a manager of emotions and situations than magistrates need to be.

Expectations

In by and large accepting the Administration's legal system, Hageners have tried to adapt it and make notions and procedures derived from their knowledge of official dispute-settlement relevant at an infra-curial level. This is one reason why it is so irrelevant for Europeans to dismiss unofficial courts as the simple counterparts of private, out-of-court mediations in their own societies. In fact, councillors and komiti often try to apply 'legal' precepts in domestic contexts and to other situations where the last thing a European might expect was reference to the 'law'. They make no sharp contrast between the concerns of official and unofficial courts. Shack (1969) describes how, in Ethiopia, courts run by Gurage tribesmen deal mainly with readjusting social relations between members of the tribes, while government courts deal with matters arising from government edicts. Hageners use government courts to introduce sanctions into dealings with their kinsmen and neighbours. But in order to make the new procedures and notions workable, they have had to graft them onto, and have them supported by, those traditional processes

---

[1] This is discussed in A.M. Strathern (in press).

which already provided a framework for peaceful settlement. A result of this is a Hagen tendency to assume that the aims of unofficial and official courts are more or less identical: they attribute to the judiciary functions it cannot perform, and misinterpret the powers with which many officials are invested.

Substantively this gives rise to two major areas of dissatisfaction with the official judicial system, which appear to contradict each other. Thus, on the one hand, Hageners may seek from persons holding an official court a much broader interest in the ramifications of a trouble case than it is within the official's competence to have, hoping perhaps for some authoritative recognition of the need for reconciliation; on the other hand, they may desire the firmness and absoluteness of a court decision from persons who can do nothing more than attempt reconciliation. As it seemed in 1970, their ideal would perhaps be a unitary system which dealt with a whole range of civil as well as criminal complaints, and which combined the authority of officialdom and its powerful sanctions with a flexibility which would allow officials to set cases into their social context. This, of course, is what in miniature their unofficial courts provide.

A central emphasis of the unofficial court is on the more or less complete settlement of a dispute, through investigating the issues which have created grievances in the disputants, bringing these to light, pinpointing the 'root of the trouble', and restoring as far as possible relationships damaged by the affair. At the same time, unofficial courts are also concerned with the ways wrongs have offended certain values, and they reinforce the definition of particular acts according to whether they are socially desirable or not. The maintenance of social order (disruption of as few relations as possible) may as a value here override other considerations, such as an exact assessment of responsibility and intention.[1]

Hageners do have a concept of individual responsibility, but believe that to establish the facts of guilt does not lead to an automatic solution of all disputes. Their contrast between responsibility for an act and liability to make amends for it, derived from the jural status of the disputants, does not only put children in a special category, but also women, and also sometimes a man's clansmen or other kinsmen, depending on the details of a case. Admission of responsibility and liability must be expressed in some transaction which will afford satisfaction to those with a grievance. A fairly wide definition of jural liability may make

---

[1] Which can be done only when a narrow view is taken of the issues in question.

the question of malevolent intention unimportant. Hageners recognise that acts can be committed by persons in a state of emotional stress, through mental aberration, and through carelessness, and such factors may be taken into account where the dispute is one of low inflammability. But if the issue is interpreted in terms of political provocation, especially where an act is seen as aggression by one group against another, the circumstances of its happening often become irrelevant in relation to other conflicts it precipitates. A situation of 'absolute responsibility' arises.[1] Finally, 'settlement' may seem to be more important than the rights of individuals. Certain traditionally disadvantaged categories of persons, primarily women vis-a-vis men and low-status men vis-a-vis big-men, remain at a disadvantage in the unofficial courts, as far as the ease with which they can obtain a hearing or present their own point of view in a persuasive manner is concerned. It should also be remembered, however, that <u>komiti</u> will usually give an ear to what complaints are brought to them, and although they may decide a matter is too trivial for a full court, may be able to offer comfort if not justice.

The <u>kiap</u>'s handling of trouble cases in the past combined both a concern for public order and a capacity to deal with offences. In fact, these derived from different aspects of his roles (administrator and magistrate), but it meant that he 'settled disputes' roughly along lines familiar to Hageners. The paradox is that although the modern official courts are ostensibly concerned with law and order, they fail in Hageners' eyes to take cognisance of matters directly related to both of these elements. Increasing official specialisation has led to a point where these courts deal with offences, while <u>kiap</u> have to prevent tribal fighting. This dissociation results in a questioning of where the power lies.

On a large scale, Hageners' concern for 'settlement' leads them to take into account the political context and possible ramifications of issues concerning different clans or tribes; while on a small scale it shows in the consideration given to people who have grievances to air, and in the desire to 'excavate all the talk' so that further troubles are forestalled. Supreme Court silence on some of the political implications of homicide may be as puzzling as, if more serious than, the restrictions of a Local Court hearing. Hageners sometimes feel that such a hearing has been superficial, that little effort has been expended on testing the statements of the defendants, and that as there is no arena

---

[1] See, for example, Gluckman's general discussion of this concept in relation to Barotse jurisprudence (Gluckman 1965, on the Lozi of Zambia).

for the 'true plaintiff' (e.g., an injured person) to put his point of view, the court does not always get to the 'root of the trouble'. This is in spite of the fact that in personal terms the present LCM is contrasted favourably with some previous _kiap_, as someone who does 'hear talk',[1] an image partly derived from the time-consuming trouble he spends on out-of-court mediations. When people envisage taking a tricky case to a _kiap_, they may actually express the hope that he will be able 'to find out the root of the trouble'. Only once this has been done can a proper decision follow.

While they feel not enough attention is given to the wider implications of offences, and the extent to which a particular penalty satisfies those who have suffered at the hands of the guilty man, Hageners also sometimes express a wish that penalties were more severe than they are. In being aware that modern judicial procedure is a substitute for the use of force, they perhaps seek from it some of the vindictive satisfactions which violence afforded in the past. One hears stories about the extreme brutality with which police allegedly pursue their investigations and extract information about a case before an accusation is framed. Regardless of whether these stories are based on fact, their circulation among Hageners may reflect something of the latter's preoccupation with problems of violence. They have been forced to cope with and suppress such physical impulses of their own. This, in turn, explains why they perhaps expect more dramatic gestures from the courts than they get. Malt (in Case 8) was hoping for an emphatic acclaim of his own lawful behaviour, and many of his clansmen were hoping for an equally emphatic chastising of their opponents.

But there is more than vindictiveness to this point of view. Law and order in the European sense can be said to exist if violent behaviour is controlled; but Hageners tend to think that if feelings are not also brought under control, settlement has been illusory. This lies behind the attention given to matters, perhaps in a narrow view extraneous to an offence, which are pertinent to the attitudes of offender and offended. Notions of revenge are prominent in Hagen thinking, and settlements have to cope with feelings relating to such notions. In unofficial courts the person with a grievance must be seen to be satisfied. Most Hageners would say that someone who publicly accepts payment has no further legitimate grounds for taking vengeance. In this

---

[1] Ordinary people may criticise councillors as tending to abruptness in their imitation of _kiap_. 'Now with councillors the talk is cut short' (for a different view, see pp.133-4).

context it is perhaps unfortunate that the Local Court makes so little use of its powers to award compensation in criminal cases.

The network of agencies which deals with civil complaints 'out of court' does not really provide satisfaction in these terms. Although persons are allowed to say all they have to say or are recommended to accept mutual compensation payments, this is done in an inappropriate context. Hageners usually take cases to officials in the hope of mobilising sanctions. The points of dispute often have already been argued out, and what the participants look for is the kind of arbitrary dispute-terminating judgment they are used to from Local Court hearings. The LCM probably affords most satisfaction in this context since he can convert an out-of-court mediation into a civil hearing at his own discretion. Hageners are aware of the superior sanctions (jail, police action and so on) officials wield in criminal proceedings by comparison with those their own councillors have; but they also tend to attribute to the former the same personal 'strength' which the latter must evince in order to settle disputes at home and expect the authorities to display such 'strength' on all occasions. They may be disappointed by the inconclusiveness of an interview with the welfare officer or kiap, especially if the matter involves marriage or divorce. The success of the LCM in mediations, we have seen, is largely derived from the fact that little distinction is made by Hageners between his magisterial and out-of-court roles; were he to pronounce more emphatically on marriage cases than he sometimes does, his word would probably be accepted as it is in criminal proceedings.

For it is unfortunate that troubles arising from marital difficulties tend to be officially relegated not just to the domain of civil adjustment, but to processes which are so very informal. At the Mt Hagen court-house in 1970,[1] disputes bearing on marriage had to compete for the attention of a magistrate at the end of a long day of hearing criminal cases. Not only did the fact that no specific time was set aside for mediation[2] to some extent make a mockery of the ostensible advantages of mediation (that grievances

---

[1] Since this date the enlargement of the court-house staff in Mt Hagen has ensured that more time is made available to handle these cases. I do not know what proportion are filed as civil complaints and what proportion are heard out of court.

[2] Something the councillors were campaigning for, and which the LCM ideally would have liked to provide. Komiti were complaining in 1970 that all the LCM's time was taken up with plis kot to the neglect of kot bilong mipela (the 'civil' cases they were trying to bring to the LCM).

be heard as fully as possible), but many disputes had reached a point at which they needed shaping by some relatively formal court process. Further referrals by the official in some cases simply led to the disputes being dropped (not settled) through inertia.

It may be that in European society family troubles can be effectively insulated from other areas of social life, and dealt with as 'private' issues. In Hagen wide-reaching disputes may develop from apparently trivial domestic beginnings, and matters arising from bridewealth, divorce, and conjugal and affinal difficulties constituted an extremely large area of traditional litigation. They seem to be matters over which appeals have been made for official intervention for a long time (thus as early as 1956 an attempt was made to put a ceiling on bridewealth amounts, 'an idea of the natives themselves'[1]). It makes small sense in Hagen terms to treat these matters as a special category. Moreover, whatever readiness there is on the part of bodies such as the welfare office to listen to women's complaints,[2] one might have thought that refusal to handle these issues formally could lead to some of the injustices which magistrates are so anxious to avoid in other contexts (as Smithers 1963:221-2 notes). It is certainly true that Hagen men sometimes classify marriage disputes as 'rubbish' troubles caused by females,[3] but there would seem to be no real reason why this should also be the official attitude. And since this is an area of dispute in which women are most likely to be involved (by contrast with crimes of violence, theft, drinking, and so on), once again it would seem that women are placed at a disadvantage.

As far as criminal matters are concerned, however, it is nowadays perhaps easier for women and other underprivileged persons to make effective complaints. Although not very often, women are sometimes seen outside the police station reporting beatings they have received from their menfolk. Probably the very plethora of agencies dealing with disputes means that a greater proportion of issues are 'settled' these days, since one of the traditional solutions - withdrawal and refusal to meet one's opponents to discuss the matter - has become a more remote possibility. It is not simply that the agencies themselves contribute directly by

---

[1] Patrol report, Western Highlands District 146, Hagen 8-56/57. Council rules relating to bridewealths were not finally gazetted until about 1970.

[2] See Chapter 3.

[3] A categorisation taken to extremes in a recent (1972) dogmatic refusal of some Dei councillors to give any heed to disputes brought up by women.

presenting solutions, but their presence acts as a catalyst to home settlement. Suggestions that cases be taken to an outside body can work as an effective threat in situations where people see there would be a real advantage in having the matter dealt with by local councillors or komiti. The issue of a court summons on a civil complaint may be enough to impel disputants to reach agreement, without having to undergo a hearing before the LCM. At the same time, individuals are also more likely to pursue their complaints beyond the councillor or komiti because they feel they can get further hearings elsewhere. The more accessible the police, LCM, welfare officer and such are, the lower becomes the threshold at which people bypass the unofficial court if they receive no satisfaction from it. Here an individual's chances of seeking 'justice' in personal terms may be at the expense of a rapid 'settlement' of the issue within his community.

One effect of Administration agencies as a whole (including the courts system) is to encourage the expression of personal rights and to devalue efforts to solve problems in relationships. Hageners always recognised that a balance had to be maintained between pushing one's own claims and recognising the claims of others upon one's consideration. The presence of relatively impersonal institutions allows individuals to stress their rights beyond what others might judge reasonable. For example, it was traditionally regarded as legitimate for a woman to complain if her husband decided to take a second wife without informing her, but given the validity of polygyny this in itself could not have precipitated a judicial inquiry. This is precisely what, in their eyes, takes place when a woman goes with her grievances to the welfare office. Indeed, the fact that dispute-settlement is not the main focus of official courts may lead an offender to take refuge in its processes, so that he voluntarily gives himself up to the police or whoever because he can thereby avoid having to come to terms with the persons he has injured. The court comes between disputants, so that although a plaintiff may be pleased at the punishment meted out to the offender, the offender can say that he has to pay because he broke the law, rather than because he hurt so-and-so.[1] Having suffered punishment, he may then feel no obligation to make private amends afterwards, and these are in fact rarely demanded. It is certainly not possible to characterise official court procedure as in an overall way more punitive or unpleasant than settlement at home; there may be situations

---

[1] Gulliver (1963:274) notes that introduced courts among the Arusha of East Africa hold attractions for 'those who wish to attempt to avoid the necessity of compliance with the pressures and sanctions of their associates'.

where the offender considers that it offers him very definite advantages. A jail sentence is certainly regarded as an intent to punish, but its unpleasantness is judged in relative terms against the gravity of the crime.

The official judiciary performs a very real function in relation to one class of disputes. These are troubles which have been exhaustively argued over and reached genuine deadlock. The parties may have come to a point where they would welcome an authoritative decision, however arbitrary, to just 'cut' the issue. In these contexts it is probably an advantage, rather than the reverse, for the magistrate to have only a sketchy knowledge of the factors involved. Indeed, in some dilemmas an individual may seek from an official the decision he himself is unable to make, so that he will be satisfied whichever way it falls. Many potential divorce suits come into this category. The cause of divorce was traditionally often blamed on the wife; a husband whose own feelings are ambivalent may use an appeal to the LCM - for he either gains back his wife without having to plead with her, or else gets rid of her without having to lose face or, according to Hagen rules (too complicated to enumerate here), forfeit return of bridewealth. In many situations one hears people suggesting, 'We'll take the matter to the kiap and see what he has to say'. In this context very different requirements may be made of officials in contrast to local councillors. A councillor may be hampered, as the protagonists are, by their knowledge of what lies behind particular complaints, whereas Administration agencies can be asked to provide simple judgments as they also provide other directives for behaviour.

A parallel function of the unofficial courts lies in the extent to which 'settlements', even at the expense of equally gross mishandlings of individual rights, can prevent the escalation of disputes. Political repercussions of the type which in the past would have led to warfare can often, though not always, be damped down in early stages. This is probably one of the major administrative, if not judicial, achievements of the unofficial courts.

Conclusion

The relationship between official and unofficial courts is relevant not only to the way in which new ideas have been introduced to and absorbed by this highlands society, but to the whole question of how far the Administration is also accorded some legitimacy.[1]

---

[1] Or 'legality' in one of the senses in which Barnes (1969) uses it during his discussion of colonial legal processes in eastern Zambia.

We have seen discrepancies between Hageners' model of the legal system and the Administration's, and discrepancies in the actual way in which official and unofficial courts approach offences and disputes. The Hageners' model represents to some extent an attempt to accommodate both the notion of law and order and the sovereignty of an introduced government. Instead of isolating and withdrawing themselves, dismissing 'law' as something relevant only to official courts, they have mentally structured the present state of affairs so that they themselves and their leaders can behave as though their courts were part of the official system, and something of the role of _kiap_ devolves upon councillors. Councillors and _komiti_ in this light become mouthpieces for what they interpret to be _kiap_ law. Nevertheless, councillors and _komiti_ are aware of differences between themselves and Europeans: while they all uphold a single law, officials have powers of enforcement which they lack. They are keenly aware of this, and 'borrow' as much power as possible. As far as the legal system is concerned, the _kiap_ (and he is the prototype 'official') is seen as much as a man of force as a man of law. This perception of power relations cannot be ignored. Behind the _kiap_ is his power to call in the police; he can threaten jail; it is remembered that some people were killed in the past. But submission to control is not the same as admission that the _kiap_ are right, and I think that, on the whole, in the context of hearing courts, Administration pronouncements have indeed become acceptable. The idea of law is also attractive: it has positive value in a situation of enforced peace because of its dual associations - with ideas of progress and modernism and with traditional norms relating to peaceful dispute-settlement. 'Law' does not remain an abstract concept, but can be manipulated in social situations, and thus it acquires value. Only when major political issues blow up and the official system is patently inadequate to cope with problems which Hageners think are there, is the Administration's legitimacy to act questioned. Yet since the idea of law is so closely related to the idea of sanctions, there is a danger that if the higher courts of the official judicial system come to appear less meaningful, the Local Court and then the unofficial courts will also lose effectiveness. _Kiap_ and other magistrates are strangers, but Hageners take their cases to them because they are powerful; councillors and _komiti_ are not powerful to the same degree, but have the advantage of not being strangers. At present, I doubt if appeals to nothing more than 'the law' would make Hageners accept for long the adjudication of strangers who could not also demonstrate they possessed power.

That the LCM, _kiap_ and other officials are so readily equated with one another in some aspects, arises not only from Hageners' failure to appreciate the constitutional importance of a separation of powers, but from a positive recognition that all these persons, in their different jobs, are contributing to 'government' in its widest sense. The LCM is seen to be powerful because he is part of the government. As government agents at a lower level, councillors and komiti interpret their position as encompassing the same range of functions as is distributed among various Administration officials. Thus their judicial activities are regarded by the people as a fundamental part of the process of local government. In the conversation quoted[1] between councillor Malt and an official, the councillor practically said that keeping people law-abiding was a matter of local government, and what was his own job if it were not precisely to do with that?

It is clear that Hageners have not grasped the importance of many of the procedural rules belonging to the imposed legal system, nor the nature of its constitution. It is also true that in its continued insistence on the illegality of councillors' actions in holding courts the Administration does not realise perhaps to what extent the notion of 'law and order' is potentially acceptable. Reay (1970:546) has written of political advancement that it 'can be more fruitfully assessed through examining the acceptance or rejection of particular political ideas than the presence or absense of legitimacy in respect of total political systems'. It seems that Hageners' absorption of judicial and legal ideas may be assessed on both fronts. On the one hand, the judicial idea of 'law' has wide currency; on the other, the total legal system, it is arguable, does indeed have legitimacy for them. But paradoxically its legitimacy derives from the fact that it has been restructured in the minds of Hageners themselves. The very nature of their perception of it, as involving komiti and councillors as well as kiap, bulwarks acceptance of the Administration in this sphere. Such factors partly account for the plethora of disputes brought to the notice of officials, which can be predicted to increase as the agencies expand. Paradoxically this contributes to the Administration's growing concern with 'lawlessness'. It is the same paradox which leads to councillors being blamed for holding 'courts' or imposing 'fines'. For these are direct products of Hageners' efforts to make some of the introduced judicial notions relevant to themselves. Since they see no reason why 'law' should not be applicable to even the most minor disputes, they endow persons who take an obvious interest in community matters with the right to administer it.

The crux of the matter is this: what weight is to be given to the legality or illegality of Hageners' own attempts to respond positively to the new law? For there can be a genuine acceptance of principles without full endorsement of or even understanding

---

[1] See p.116.

of procedure.[1] Hageners are oversanguine in their view of a single judicial hierarchy, in that they attribute functions to parts of it which it cannot successfully discharge. The question is whether the irritations arising from the gap between the Hageners' and the Administration's models can be ignored as the price of the present accommodation between the people of Hagen and the sovereignty of the Administration, or whether reforms of some kind, even on a local or District scale, should be introduced. The question has to be posed since there is a possibility that one of the requirements that will be made of an independent government will be proof of its legitimacy to rule.

[1] Again see Reay (1970).

Appendix

Some implications

> ... the judgment of posterity is ... likely to be concerned with the capacity of the government of an independent Papua New Guinea to establish a stable regime and to maintain public order. Oram (in press)

> To deny recognition to regular local usages on that ground alone [that a practice enjoying limited application would not be in the interest of a law common to the whole country] would be to make a blind bargain at the cost of a feasible, if humbler, one. (B.J. Brown 1971:247)

Barnett (1969:175) suggests that two factors influencing the effectiveness of Local Court orders are the degree to which they 'are accepted by local communities and ... accord with native custom and contemporary public opinion'. To this one could add a third point: the extent to which people not very clear about the constitution of the courts attribute to the Local Court different powers and functions from those it actually possesses - so that its recommendations are further judged by this standard of expectations.

The kinds of expectations which Hageners have about what an effective dispute-settling institution should achieve are extremely relevant to any consideration of reforms which could affect them. Two factors, in particular, would have to be balanced carefully. First, we have seen how councillors and _komiti_, who conduct the unofficial courts, express concern about what sanctions they can use. There is a case for making constitutional alterations to invest them with quasi-magisterial power;[1] but the danger is that they might become too much like the present magistrates. For the second factor is that, although councillors and _komiti_ compare themselves with _kiap_ and the LCM, much of their success comes from an ability to work within a neotraditional framework of assumptions about the process and purpose of dispute-settlement, and from their detailed information about the histories of persons and groups.[2]

I am not sure that it would be feasible to completely transform the present roles of councillors and _komiti_ and outlaw the kinds of jobs they now do. I am thinking here of such possibilities as the creation of a panel of Hagen 'magistrates', below the level of the Local Court, to act as a tribunal in hearing cases. If the 'magistrates' were selected from all over a council area, they would be regarded by Europeans as able to give relatively disinterested though knowledgeable opinions; but it is doubtful to what extent such a proposal would work for Hageners if it meant that other councillors and _komiti_ were forbidden to hold courts at all. A tribunal of this kind might, however, be workable as a court of appeal. Were _komiti_ or councillors to be invested individually with some degree of authority (as _kiap_ can be), a tribunal might very well sit to consider appeals from the judgments of these persons. It would probably be too big a step (and too unmanageable) to have

---

1 Cf. Barnett (1969:179), also Guise (1971:50).

2 Which is rather more than simply a general knowledge of 'Hagen custom'.

people, in the first instance, take their troubles to a panel of comparative strangers, but a reasonable requirement that a councillor's or komiti's recommendations be open to scrutiny by his colleagues. If the dismantling of the councillor's portmanteau (A.J. Strathern 1970:565) is desirable, it would be an appropriate division of labour for komiti to act with quasi-magisterial authority in hearing cases while a panel of councillors drawn from all over the council area considered their decisions when these were questioned.

B.J. Brown (1971) suggests ways in which a new Local Court might be developed. While the District Court remains a forum for litigants lacking common cultural background (and by which defendants would be free to choose to be heard), he would incorporate into the Local Court a panel of assessors drawn from the local population. But it would not replace 'out-of-court' mediation. He does suggest that Local Court mediation procedures themselves be formalised to some extent (e.g., in the recognition of minor criminal offences as 'amenable to such a process'),[1] but the idea would be 'to leave native conciliation procedures well alone' (B.J. Brown 1971:249). Yet this is not a very practical aim to apply to a situation where those who try to achieve settlement through 'native conciliation procedures' in fact rely in part on a supposed connection with the official judicial system. Solutions at the level of the Local Court would tackle only half the problem in Hagen. The other half lies in how the infra-curial structure (of unofficial courts) - which exists, is used, is thought to be part of the official structure - should relate to the officially constituted courts.

It is possible, however, to leave to one side the whole question of major constitutional rearrangements and still consider a few minor ways in which the position of komiti in their capacity as dispute-settlers could be strengthened and 'legalised'. (i) The Administration could recognise their de facto adjudication in minor criminal as well as civil matters. (ii) In civil cases,[2] the process of referral from komiti to official magistrate could be regularised, once komiti were recognised as assisting the judicial process in a formal rather than informal way. For instance, specific periods of time (days of the week) could be set aside for the hearing of issues which komiti wished to bring to the notice of the LCM. One might want also to preserve the present safeguard of individual access to the LCM but rule that once an individual submitted to a komiti's court, his complaint could be transferred to a higher authority only by appealing against a previous decision (rather than by his manipulating an alternative process). This would have the effect of giving the komiti's decisions some standing for they would be open to official scrutiny.[3] (iii) It would have the further effect of still allowing civil cases to be handled 'out of court', but treating them formally once they were brought into the Local Court. An appeal against a komiti's decision by litigants would have to be differentiated from instances where a komiti himself referred to the LCM cases he could not settle. If several attempts had already been made to reach a solution in some difficult case the magistrate might, in a civil court capacity, inquire into these attempts as part of evidence of the extent to which the parties were eager for a settlement. (iv) In criminal cases, investigations by the police could also take into account previous komiti courts concerning the offender (compilation of an offender's record in this way could be made relevant to the imposition of penalty without having to affect the process of judgment). (v) Komiti might be given the authority, perhaps by council rules, to recommend compensation payments (refusal to comply being decided by appeal to the Local Court) or impose fines up to some specified amount (which could go into council funds). The sanctions of imprisonment and of substantial fines could remain

---

[1] See also Barnett (1969:171).

[2] For recommendations concerning abolition of a distinction between criminal and civil offences, see B.J. Brown (1971:253-4), Barnett (in press).

[3] A LCM sitting on such a case might lean heavily on a panel of assessors (cf. the present duty councillors) in judging the komiti's decision.

within the power of the Local Court. Councils might also be encouraged to formulate rules relating to the imposition of compensation payments which could be administered by komiti. (vi) In view of the amount of time which komiti are likely to continue to spend as professionals on their judicial duties, councils could possibly debate again the question of an honorarium for these men. (vii) Finally, the Local Court itself could perhaps mirror more closely some of the processes fundamental to komiti courts, thereby giving these further weight. It could use its present power to make compensation awards, which would in turn mean that the magistrate would have to inquire into the circumstances of and relationships between complainant and defendant, and perhaps assess how far the complainant felt himself injured. In focusing upon these two categories of persons as having different points of view, the police might also make more formal some of their interrogation procedures - starting from the assumption that claims and counter-claims will be made and should be recorded as such, rather than working simply under the rubric that any means are justifiable in discovering the 'facts' and 'truth' of a matter. Neither of these modifications would in any way prevent (where appropriate) the presentation of the charge to a criminal in terms of an offence against the laws of the land.

Nor as a whole would they seem to go against the spirit of Derham's recommendation, in his review of the administration of justice in Papua New Guinea for the then Minister of Territories, as quoted by Hasluck in 1961:

> that participation by the native people in the processes of justice should be as part of the regular judicial system of the Territory.[1]

---

[1] Commonwealth of Australia, Parliamentary Debates (Hansard), House of Representatives, vol.33, p.2349, 24 October 1961.

Bibliography

Archer, P., 1956. The Queen's Courts, Penguin Books, Harmondsworth.

Barnes, J.A., 1969. 'The politics of law' in Man in Africa (M. Douglas and P. Kaberry, eds), Tavistock, London.

Barnett, T.E., 1967. 'The courts and the people of Papua and New Guinea', Journal of the Papua and New Guinea Society, vol.1, no.2, pp.95-101.

-- 1969. 'The Local Court Magistrate and the settlement of disputes' in Fashion of Law in New Guinea (B.J. Brown, ed.) pp.159-69, Butterworths, Sydney.

-- in press. 'A lawyer's perspective', Melanesian Law Journal.

Beattie, J., 1971. The Nyoro State, Oxford University Press, London.

Berndt, R.M., 1962. Excess and Restraint. Social Control among a New Guinea Mountain People. University of Chicago Press, Illinois.

Brown, B.J., 1969. 'Justice and the edge of law: towards a "people's court"' in Fashion of Law in New Guinea (B.J. Brown, ed.), pp.181-215, Butterworths, Sydney.

-- 1971. 'Outlook for law in New Guinea', Oceania, vol.41, no.4, pp.244-54.

Brown, P., 1963. 'From anarchy to satrapy', American Anthropologist, vol.65, no.1, pp.1-15.

Bulmer, R.N.H., 1961. 'Kyaka bossboys: post-contact leadership in a New Guinea highland society', paper delivered to ANZAAS conference.

Bureau of Statistics, 1972. 'Papua New Guinea population census - July 1971', Preliminary Bulletin no.1, Urban Centres, Konedobu, Papua.

Colebatch, H.K. and Colebatch, C., Reay, M. and Strathern, A.J., 1971. 'Free elections in a guided democracy' in The Politics of Dependence. Papua New Guinea 1968 (A.L. Epstein, R.S. Parker and M. Reay, eds), pp.218-74, ANU Press, Canberra.

Epstein, A.L., 1967. 'The case method in the field of law' in The Craft of Social Anthropology (A.L. Epstein, ed.), pp.205-30, Tavistock, London.

-- 1969. Matupit. Land, Politics and Change among the Tolai of New Britain, ANU Press, Canberra.

-- 1970a. 'Aspects of political development on the Gazelle Peninsula' in The Politics of Melanesia (M.W. Ward, ed.), pp.105-22, UPNG and ANU, Canberra.

-- 1970b. 'Procedure in the study of customary law', Melanesian Law Journal, vol.1, no.1, pp.51-7.

-- 1971. 'Dispute settlement among the Tolai', Oceania, vol.41, no.3, pp.157-70.

Fallers, L.A., 1969. Law without Precedent. Legal Ideas in Action in the Courts of Colonial Busoga, University of Chicago Press, Illinois.

Fenbury, D., 1966. 'Kot bilong mipela', New Guinea, vol.1, no.4, pp.61-6.

Frake, C.O., 1969. 'Struck by speech: the Yakan concept of litigation' in Law in Culture and Society (L. Nader, ed.), pp.147-67, Aldine Publishing Co., Chicago.

Gluckman, M., 1955. The Judicial Process among the Barotse of Northern Rhodesia, Manchester University Press, Manchester.

-- 1965. The Ideas in Barotse Jurisprudence, Yale University Press, New Haven.

Guise, J., 1971. 'A policeman's lot', New Guinea, vol.6, no.2, pp.48-51.

Gulliver, P.H., 1963. Social Control in an African Society. A Study of the Arusha: Agricultural Masai of Northern Tanganyika, Routledge and Kegan Paul, London.

Hatanaka, S., 1972. 'Leadership and socio-economic change in Sinasina, New Guinea highlands', New Guinea Research Bulletin no.45, New Guinea Research Unit, Port Moresby and Canberra.

Hide, R.L., 1971. 'Land demarcation and disputes in the Chimbu District of the New Guinea highlands' in 'Land tenure and economic development: problems and policies in Papua New Guinea and Kenya', New Guinea Research Bulletin no.40, New Guinea Research Unit, Port Moresby and Canberra.

Kaberry, P.M., 1941-42. 'Law and political organisation in the Abelam tribe, New Guinea', Oceania, vol.12, no.1, pp.79-95; no.3, pp.209-25; no.4, pp.331-63.

Lawrence, P., 1969. 'The state versus stateless societies in Papua and New Guinea' in Fashion of Law in New Guinea (B.J. Brown, ed.), pp.15-37, Butterworths, Sydney.

Leahy, M.J. and Crain, M., 1937. The Land that Time Forgot, Hunt and Blackett, London.

Lynch, C.J., 1969. 'Aspects of political and constitutional development and allied topics' in Fashion of Law in New Guinea (B.J. Brown, ed.), pp.39-69, Butterworths, Sydney.

Mattes, C.J., 1969. 'The courts system' in Fashion of Law in New Guinea (B.J. Brown, ed.), pp.71-82, Butterworths, Sydney.

Mihalic, F., 1971. The Jacaranda Dictionary and Grammar of Melanesian Pidgin, The Jacaranda Press, Sydney.

Momis, J. and Ogan, E., 1971. 'Bougainville '71', New Guinea, vol.6, no.2, pp.32-40.

Moore, S.F., 1970. 'Politics, procedures and norms in changing Chagga law', Africa, vol.40, pp.321-43.

Nash, G., 1970. 'Legal structure and indigenous business enterprise: the need for change' in 'The indigenous role in business enterprise', New Guinea Research Bulletin no.35, pp.27-46, New Guinea Research Unit, Port Moresby and Canberra.

Ogan, E., 1972. 'Business and cargo: socio-economic change among the Nasioi of Bougainville', New Guinea Research Bulletin no.44, New Guinea Research Unit, Port Moresby and Canberra.

Ollennu, N.A., 1969. 'The structure of African judicial authority and problems of evidence and proof in traditional courts' in Ideas and Procedures in African Customary Law (M. Gluckman, ed.), pp.110-22, Oxford University Press, London.

Oram, N., 1970. 'The development of Port Moresby, what and whose are the problems', Search, vol.1, no.5, pp.282-8.

-- in press. 'Administration, development and public order' in Alternative Strategies in Papua New Guinea (A.R. Clunies Ross, ed.), Oxford University Press.

Reay, M., 1964. 'Present-day politics in the New Guinea highlands', American Anthropologist special publication: New Guinea - the Central Highlands (J.B. Watson, ed.), vol.66, no.4, part 2, pp.240-56.

-- 1970. 'Roads and bridges between three levels of politics' in The Politics of Melanesia (M.W. Ward, ed.), pp.531-48, UPNG and ANU, Canberra.

Ross, W., 1936. 'Ethnological notes on the Mount Hagen tribes', Anthropos, vol.31, pp.341-63.

Rowley, C.D., 1965. The New Guinea Villager, F.W. Cheshire, Sydney.

Sakora, B.B., 1970. 'Administration of justice at the village level', Justice, no.3, pp.11-28.

Salisbury, R.F., 1964. 'Despotism and Australian administration in the New Guinea highlands', American Anthropologist special publication: New Guinea - the Central Highlands (J.B. Watson, ed.), vol.66, no.4, part 2, pp.225-39.

Shack, W.A., 1969. 'Guilt and innocence: problem and method in the Gurage judicial system' in Ideas and Procedures in African Customary Law (M. Gluckman, ed.), pp.153-68, Oxford University Press, London.

Sinha, D.P., 1969. 'The Wurup project in the New Guinea highlands: strategies in planned change', Oceania, vol.39, no.4, pp.290-7.

Smithers, R.A., 1963. 'Law and the Territory of Papua and New Guinea', Melbourne University Law Review, vol.4, pp.212-37.

-- 1970. 'The rule of law and the administration of justice in an emerging society', The Rule of Law in an Emerging Society, report of the proceedings of the Papua and New Guinea conference held at Port Moresby, September 1965. International Commission of Jurists, Australian Section, Sydney, pp.50-82.

Strathern, A.J., 1970. 'Kiap, councillor and big-man: role-contrasts in Mount Hagen' in The Politics of Melanesia (M.W. Ward, ed.), pp.549-67, UPNG and ANU, Canberra.

-- 1971. The Rope of Moka. Big-men and Ceremonial Exchange in Mount Hagen, New Guinea, Cambridge University Press, Cambridge.

-- 1972a. One Father, One Blood. Descent and Group Structure among the Melpa People, ANU Press, Canberra.

-- 1972b. 'Political development and problems of social control in Mount Hagen', paper delivered to Sixth Waigani Seminar on 'Priorities in Melanesian Development', to be published by UPNG and ANU, Canberra.

-- in press. 'The Supreme Court: a matter of prestige and power', Melanesian Law Journal.

Strathern, A.M., 1972. Women in Between. Female Roles in a Male World: Mount Hagen, New Guinea, Seminar Press, London.

-- in press. 'The problems of a dispute-settler' in Contention and Dispute: Aspects of Law and Social Control in Melanesia (A.L. Epstein, ed.), ANU Press, Canberra.

Strauss, H. and Tischner, H., 1962. Die Mi-Kultur der Hagenberg - Stämme im Östlichen Zentral Neuguinea, Cram, de Gruyter and Co., Hamburg.

van Velsen, J., 1969. 'Procedural informality, reconciliation and false comparisons' in Ideas and Procedures in African Customary Law (M. Gluckman, ed.), pp.137-52, Oxford University Press, London.

Vicedom, G.F. and Tischner, H., 1943-48. Die Mbowamb, Die Kultur der Hagenberg - Stämme im Östlichen Zentral Neuguinea, Cram, de Gruyter and Co., Hambu g, three volumes.

Watts, J., 1972. 'Collision course', New Guinea, vol.6, no.4, pp.52-7.

Wurm, S.A., 1964. 'Australian New Guinea highlands languages and the distribution of their typological features', American Anthropologist special publication: New Guinea - the Central Highlands (J.B. Watson, ed.), vol.66, no.4, part 2, pp.77-97.

Young, M.W., 1971. Fighting with Food. Leadership, Values and Social Control in a Massim Society, Cambridge University Press, Cambridge.

Index

Abstract

New Guinea Research Bulletin
No. 47, 1972

Official and unofficial courts: legal assumptions and expectations in a highlands community

Local government councillors and their adjutants in the Hagen sub-district of the Western Highlands preside over unofficial, technically illicit courts, which they themselves regard as part of the official judicial system. They also make extensive use of government agencies to assist in settling disputes. But difficulties arise from the lack of formal recognition, as well as from the Hagen people's misinterpretation of the precise functions of official courts and from their own expectations of what dispute-settlement procedures should achieve.

New Guinea Research Bulletins

Bulletin No. 1	The Erap Mechanical Farming Project by R.G. Crocombe and G.R. Hogbin, April 1963
Bulletin No. 2	Land, Work and Productivity at Inonda by R.G. Crocombe and G.R. Hogbin, August 1963
Bulletin No. 3	Social Accounts of the Monetary Sector of the Territory of Papua and New Guinea, 1956/57 to 1960/61 by R.C. White, January 1964
Bulletin No. 4	Communal Cash Cropping among the Orokaiva by R.G. Crocombe, May 1964
Bulletin No. 5	A Survey of Indigenous Rubber Producers in the Kerema Bay Area by G.R. Hogbin, October 1964
Bulletin No. 6	The European Land Settlement Scheme at Popondetta by D.R. Howlett, April 1965
Bulletin No. 7	The M'buke Co-operative Plantation by R.G. Crocombe, August 1965
Bulletin No. 8	Cattle, Coffee and Land among the Wain by Graham Jackson, December 1965
Bulletin No. 9	An Integrated Approach to Nutrition and Society: the Case of the Chimbu, ed. E. Hipsley, January 1966
Bulletin No.10	The Silanga Resettlement Project by Olga van Rijswijck, February 1966
Bulletin No.11	Land Tenure and Land Use among the Mount Lamington Orokaiva by Max Rimoldi, April 1966
Bulletin No.12	Education Through the Eyes of an Indigenous Urban Elite by Karol van der Veur and Penelope Richardson, August 1966
Bulletin No.13	Orokaiva Papers: Miscellaneous Papers on the Orokaiva of North East Papua, November 1966
Bulletin No.14	Rabia Camp: a Port Moresby Migrant Settlement by Nancy E. Hitchcock and N.D. Oram, January 1967
Bulletin No.15	Bulolo: a History of the Development of the Bulolo Region, New Guinea by Allan Healy, February 1967
Bulletin No.16	Papuan Entrepreneurs: Papers by R.G. Crocombe, W.J. Oostermeyer and Joanne Gray, J.V. Langmore, April 1967
Bulletin No.17	Land Tenure Conversion in the Northern District of Papua by David Morawetz, May 1967
Bulletin No.18	Social and Economic Relationships in a Port Moresby Canoe Settlement by N.D. Oram, July 1967
Bulletin No.19	A Benefit Cost Analysis of Resettlement in the Gazelle Peninsula by S. Singh, September 1967
Bulletin No.20	New Guinea People in Business and Industry: Papers from the First Waigani Seminar, December 1967
Bulletin No.21	Teachers in the Urban Community by Penelope Richardson and Karol van der Veur, January 1968
Bulletin No.22	Papers on the Papua-New Guinea House of Assembly by Norman Meller, January 1968

Bulletin No.23	Mixed-race Society in Port Moresby by B.G. Burton-Bradley, March 1968
Bulletin No.24	The Organisation of Production and Distribution among the Orokaiva by E.W. Waddell and P.A. Krinks, September 1968
Bulletin No.25	A Survey of Village Industries in Papua-New Guinea by R. Kent Wilson, November 1968
Bulletin No.26	The Contribution of Voluntary Aid Organisations to the Development of Papua-New Guinea, 1966-67, by Micheline Dewdney, January 1969
Bulletin No.27	New Guinean Entrepreneurs by B.R. Finney, February 1969
Bulletin No.28	Namasu: New Guinea's Largest Indigenous-owned Company by I.J. Fairbairn, March 1969
Bulletin No.29	Hohola: the Significance of Social Networks in Urban Adaptation of Women by Lynn Oeser, June 1969
Bulletin No.30	Inter-tribal Relations of the Maenge People of New Britain by M. Panoff, July 1969
Bulletin No.31	Inter-ethnic Marriage in New Guinea by A.W. Lind, August 1969
Bulletin No.32	New Guinea Social Science Field Research and Publications, 1962-67 by Susan C. Reeves and May Dudley, October 1969
Bulletin No.33	The Rigo Road: a Study of the Economic Effects of New Road Construction by Marion W. Ward, January 1970
Bulletin No.34	People and Planning in Papua and New Guinea: Papers by D.J. van de Kaa, J.M. Stanhope, T.S. Epstein, N.H. Fry, and C.L. Beltz, April 1970
Bulletin No.35	The Indigenous Role in Business Enterprise: Three Papers from the Third Waigani Seminar, 1969 by A.J. O'Connor, T.S. Epstein and G. Nash, May 1970
Bulletin No.36	Australia and the United Nations: New Guinea Trusteeship Issues from 1946 to 1966 by W.E. Tomasetti, July 1970
Bulletin No.37	Port Moresby Urban Development by J.V. Langmore and N.D. Oram, September 1970
Bulletin No.38	Land Tenure in West Irian: Papers by K.W. Galis, J.V. de Bruyn, J. Pouwer, J.W. Schoorl, and J. Verschueren, December 1970
Bulletin No.39	The Situm and Gobari Ex-servicemen's Settlements by A. Ploeg, January 1971
Bulletin No.40	Land Tenure and Economic Development: Problems and Policies in New Guinea and Kenya: Papers by S. Rowton Simpson, R.L. Hide, A.M. Healy, and J.K. Kinyanjui, March 1971
Bulletin No.41	Would-be Entrepreneurs? A Study of Motivation in New Guinea by Ruth S. Finney, May 1971
Bulletin No.42	Population Growth and Socio-economic Change: Papers from the Second Demography Seminar, Port Moresby 1970, September 1971
Bulletin No.43	Langandrowa and M'buke, Corporate Indigenous Plantations by A.M. McGregor, December 1971
Bulletin No.44	Business and Cargo: Socio-economic change among the Nasioi of Bougainville by E. Ogan, 1972
Bulletin No.45	Leadership and Socio-economic Change in Sinasina by Sachiko Hatanaka, 1972

Bulletin No.46 Melanesians' Choice: Tadhimboko Participation in the Solomon Islands Cash Economy by I.Q. Lasaqa, 1972

Bulletin No.47 Official and Unofficial Courts: Legal Assumptions and Expectations in a Highlands Community by Marilyn Strathern, 1972

The above bulletins are available at $1.50 each (except for Nos 24 and 46 which are $2) from the A.N.U. Press, The Australian National University, P.O. Box 4, Canberra, A.C.T., 2600, Australia, and the New Guinea Research Unit, The Australian National University, P.O. Box 1238, Boroko, Papua New Guinea.

An annual payment of $7.00 entitles the subscriber to all bulletins issued in the year.